Cyprus

by Robert Bulmer

Robert Bulmer lived in Cyprus for many years.
He returns often, to walk in the hills, explore
again the towns and villages or simply luxuriate
on the beaches. His book *Days Out in Cyprus*,
published by himself, was followed by the AA's
first edition of *Essential Cyprus* and then by
AA Thomas Cook *Travellers Cyprus*.

Above: *Kyrenia harbour*

AA Publishing

Above: *bust of the Greek Cypriot hero Archbishop Makarios outside St Michael Trypiotis in Nicosia*

Find out more about AA Publishing and the wide range of travel publications and services the AA provides by visiting our website at www.theAA.com

Written by Robert Bulmer

First published 1998. Reprinted Mar 1999
Second edition 2000. Reprinted Apr, Aug and Oct 2000, Jun 2001
Reprinted Apr 2002. Information verified and updated
Reprinted Oct 2002. This edition 2004

© Automobile Association Developments Limited 1998, 2000, 2002
Maps © Automobile Association Developments Limited 1998, 2002

Published by AA Publishing, a trading name of Automobile Association Developments Limited, whose registered office is Millstream, Maidenhead Road, Windsor, Berkshire SL4 5GD. Registered number 1878835.

Automobile Association Developments Limited retains the copyright in the original edition © 1998 and all subsequent editions, reprints and amendments.

Colour separation: BTB Digital Imaging Limited, Whitchurch, Hampshire

Printed and bound in Italy by Printer Trento S.r.l.

A01641

Contents

About this Book

KEY TO SYMBOLS

✚	map reference to the maps found in the What to See section (see below)
✉	address or location
☎	telephone number
🕐	opening times
🍴	restaurant or café on premises or nearby
Ⓜ	nearest underground train station
🚌	nearest bus/tram route
🚆	nearest overground train station
💼	ferry crossings and excursions by boat
✈	travel by air
ℹ	tourist information
♿	facilities for visitors with disabilities
✋	admission charge
↔	other places of interest nearby
❓	other practical information
▶	indicates the page where you will find a fuller description

This book is divided into five sections to cover the most important aspects of your visit to Cyprus.

Viewing Cyprus pages 5–14
An introduction to Cyprus by the author
    Cyprus's Features
    Essence of Cyprus
    The Shaping of Cyprus
    Peace and Quiet
    Cyprus's Famous

Top Ten pages 15–26
The author's choice of the Top Ten places to visit in Cyprus, each with practical information

What to See pages 27–90
The five main areas of Cyprus, each with its own brief introduction and an alphabetical listing of the main attractions
    Practical information
    Snippets of 'Did You Know…' information
    5 suggested walks
    5 suggested drives
    2 features

Where To... pages 91–116
Detailed listings of the best places to eat, stay, shop, take the children and be entertained

Practical Matters pages 117–24
A highly visual section containing essential travel information

Maps
All map references are to the individual maps found in the What to See section of this guide.
For example, Kourion has the reference
✚ 28B1 – indicating the page on which the map is located and the grid square in which the site is to be found. A list of the maps that have been used in this travel guide can be found in the index.

Prices
Where appropriate, an indication of the cost of an establishment is given by **£** signs:
£££ denotes higher prices, **££** denotes average prices, while **£** denotes lower charges.

Star Ratings
Most of the places described in this book have been given a separate rating:

✪✪✪	Do not miss
✪✪	Highly recommended
✪	Worth seeing

Viewing
Cyprus

Above: *Temple of Apollo,*
Kourion
Right: *wedding party*
at Agía Napa

Robert Bulmer's Cyprus

Travel Restrictions
This guide deals with all of Cyprus, a divided land. Visitors should appreciate that they must commit themselves to either the Greek (south) or Turkish (north) part for their stay, as movement between the two sectors is strictly limited to one crossing point from south to north with return on the same day. Readers interested in Greek Cyprus should concentrate on the chapters covering the Larnaka, Limassol, Pafos and High Troodos areas; those wishing to visit Turkish Cyprus should read the Famagusta and the North section. Nicosia is partly in the Turkish area and partly in the Greek area.

In Cyprus the oranges come straight from the tree

Cyprus, within sight of Asia Minor, is halfway to the Orient. Yet it looks westwards, attracting many visitors from Europe and aspiring to membership of the European Union. A legacy of British colonial rule is the excellent English, spoken island-wide. Western ideas are very well received. Nevertheless, Cyprus remains different and retains its own culture. This complex mixture stems from its location and history. Over the centuries Cyprus has been controlled by most great Mediterranean powers and the people have a diverse, if not exotic, ancestry.

The separation of the island today is an indirect consequence of the arrival of the Ottoman Turks in the 16th century. It is not a division easily ignored – United Nations soldiers and Greek and Turkish flags are everywhere along the Green Line. Nevertheless few visitors dwell on the political situation. Understandably they have other distractions.

In the south there are 340km of coast to explore, along with the fascinating Troodos Mountains and the towns of Larnaka, Limassol, Pafos and Nicosia. Visitors in the north have to be content with long unspoilt shores, including the fabled Karpasia peninsula and the magnificent Kyrenian Hills. The remarkable Mesaoria is there for good measure.

Where the friendliness of the people comes from is something of a mystery. Middle Eastern tradition demands hospitality for travellers, but in Cyprus it goes further – guests can be fed to bursting and an enduring memory for many visitors is the simple generosity of the islanders.

Cyprus's Features

Geography

• The island has two significant mountain ranges. Troodos in the centre reaches 1,951m, high enough to ensure snow cover in winter; the Kyrenia range, at 1,046m, is in the Turkish controlled part of the island.

• There are approximately 3,350 hours of sunshine a year, with little chance of rain between May and October.

• The sheep cope with the shortage of grazing in the dry summer by storing fat in their tails.

It is a hard life for sheep in summer; these are heading for grazing in the Avgas Gorge

Population

• The first sign of human habitation dates from 11,000 years ago.

• The island's population is 725,000, of whom about 576,000 are Greek Cypriots and 134,000 Turkish Cypriots, about 18 per cent of the total.

• The dowry system was made illegal in 1994.

Economic Factors

• Forty-six per cent of the land area is cultivated, the main crops being cereals, potatoes and citrus fruits.

• Cyprus has the third-highest standard of living in the Mediterranean. The average income here is twice as high as it is in Greece.

• A dam-building programme has increased water capacity from 6 million cu m in 1961 to 300 million in 2001. A desalination plant at Dhekalia provides 20 million litres a day.

Tourism

• The island attracts over 2 million visitors a year and tourism provides employment for some 35,000 people or 13 per cent of the workforce.

Climate Extremes
Cyprus in summer is a hot place, certainly the hottest of the Mediterranean islands, and, of course, sun worshippers love it. It is difficult to imagine that winter days can be cool and wet with snow falling on the highest ground, creating a winter wonderland among the pine trees.

Essence of Cyprus

The coffee shop, a male preserve, does not have the history of a Roman column, but it has a remarkable capacity to resist change

Cyprus is a land of contour and light – hills, valleys and plains. Beaches there are, although not endless sands along the shore. The heat of summer robs the land of life: winter rains restore spectacular colour. With its archaeological wonders Cyprus is certainly the stuff of tourist literature.

But what of the less tangible Cyprus? There is the interesting first journey to the hotel, with screeching brakes and tyres. Less disconcerting are the marvellous alfresco gastronomic events under awnings at lunch time and the stars at night. Walks through the pine forests of the high mountains will long be remembered, as will the friendliness of the people.

THE **10** ESSENTIALS

If you only have a short time to visit Cyprus, or would like to get a really complete picture of the island, here are the essentials:

- **Go to the Roman theatre at Kourion** (▶ 18–19) for a classical drama: the atmosphere is electric. Performances are held regularly throughout the summer, details from the tourist office.
- **Find a quiet beach**, preferably fringed with bushes or tall grasses, and take a swim long before breakfast.
- **Have a drink in a village coffee shop**. Be prepared to be ignored, but it is much more likely that someone will chance their English and start a conversation.

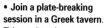

- **Have a full alfresco *meze* off the tourist track**. Be prepared to stay awake all night with a distended stomach.
- **Drive to Petra tou Romiou**, or Rock of Romios (▶ 50) in the late afternoon and stop on the cliff top a little to the east. The view is tremendous.
- **Join in a Greek dance**. The impressiveness of the steps is hardly matched by the difficulty. Take a couple of brandy sours first.

Armada of pedalos off Agía Napa

- **Join a plate-breaking session in a Greek tavern**. This mayhem is not as common as it once was, but local enquiries may lead to a venue.
- **Get invited to a village wedding**, witness the chaotic church service and drink and eat all night under the stars.
- **Ski or toboggan on Mount Olympus**. No chance here for summer visitors, the season is from 1st January to the end of March.

- **Walk a forest trail in the Troodos Mountains or Kyrenia Hills** until perspiring freely, then sit down and have a picnic.

Kourion Theatre, once a place for spectacular Roman gladiator contests, hosts a Greek wedding photo session

The Shaping of Cyprus

9000–3800 BC
First migrants arrive
from Asia Minor.
Settlements built at
Choirokoitia, Cape
Apostolos Andreas.

3800–2500 BC
Chalcolithic period.
Erimi and Lemba
became important
centres.

2500–1050 BC
Bronze Age.
Settlers arrive
from all parts of
the eastern
Mediterranean.
Alambra and
Nitovikla the
principal
locations.

700 BC
Assyria claims
control of
Cyprus.

570 BC
Egyptian
pharaoh Amasis
becomes
effective ruler of
Cyprus.

545 BC
Cyprus submits to King
Cyrus of Persia. Two
hundred years of
Persian rule follow.

325–50 BC
Cyprus becomes part of
the Greek world. The
people adopt Greek
dress and architectural
styles.

50 BC–AD 330
Cyprus under Roman
rule. The period is
marked by the building
of great amphitheatres,
baths and temples.

AD 45
Visit of the missionaries
St Barnabas and St
Paul to evangelise
Cyprus.

*King Cyrus of Persia
(550–529 BC)*

330–395
Split in Roman Empire
and the start of the
Byzantine era.

7th and 10th centuries
Arab raids.

1191
Richard the Lion-Heart,
en route to the Holy
Land, during the Third
Crusade, conquers
Cyprus and marries
Princess Berengaria in
Limassol.

1192–1489
Lusignan Rule. The great
Gothic cathedrals of
Nicosia and Famagusta
are built.

1489
Venetians,
invited to help
against
troublesome
Genoese in
Famagusta,
take island for
themselves.

1571
Ottoman Turks
realise long held
ambition to
subjugate
Cyprus.

1878
Britain, in
agreement with
Turkey, takes
control of the
island.

1914
Britain annexes Cyprus.

1955
Guerrilla campaign by
EOKA (Ethniki Organosis
Kyprion Agoniston, the
National Organisation of
Cypriot Fighters),
commences. Their aim
is to unite Cyprus with
Greece.

The British Queen inspects a guard of honour on her arrival at RAF Akrotiri

1960
Cyprus granted inde-
pendence. Archbishop
Makarios III becomes
president.

1963
Inter-communal
fighting. Turks retreat
into enclaves.

1964
United Nations soldiers
sent to keep the peace.

1974
Military coup against
Makarios, who flees.
Five days later Turkish
forces invade and take
control of north Cyprus.
Rauf Denktash
appointed leader in the
north. Makarios returns
to south Cyprus.

1975
Nicosia airport remains
under United Nations
control. Greek Cypriots
build airport at Larnaka
and begin to revive
tourist industry with
massive hotel-building
programme.

1977
Archbishop Makarios
dies and is succeeded as
president by Spirou
Kyprianou.

1983
Turks unilaterally
proclaim Republic of
Northern Cyprus.

1984
United Nations
sponsored talks end in
a stalemate.

1996
Trouble flares on the
buffer zone between
the two communities,
resulting in the deaths
of two Greek Cypriots.

1999
Cyprus accepted as a
candidate for European
Union membership.

2001
European Court of
Human Rights condems
Turkey for human rights
violations arising from
the 1974 invasion.

Peace & Quiet

Akamas's Gorges

A few companies, including Exalt Travel of Pafos (☎ 2624 3803), offer guided tours through the gorges, the Avgas being the favourite. It is something of an adventure, negotiating the boulder-strewn river bed with sheer cliffs on either side. If the weather is, or is likely to be bad, the gorges should be avoided – flash floods here can be extremely dangerous.

Cedar Valley

This is best reached from Pafos, Pano Panagía (► 67) being the last outpost before setting out on the unmetalled track into the western forest. The valley is 12km away, a good map is needed and a jeep is the best vehicle for the uncertainties ahead.

At 400m above sea level, under the canopy of trees, the air is cool. The cedars are magnificent specimens and the stillness is only likely to be disturbed by the crashing of a moufflon (wild mountain sheep) taking fright, or the trickle of water from a spring.

Western forest en route to the fabled cedars

Diarizos River

Park the car where the Pafos–Limassol road crosses the river. The turning to Palaia Pafos (► 63) is a little further east; the turning to distant Platres about 1km to the west. The stone arched pedestrian bridge is a good landmark. A track on the west bank leads, in about 2km, to the sea.

Grasses and reeds line the banks and there is a good chance of spotting purple heron and other fascinating water birds. In the dry summer months, the river is reduced to a trickle.

Famagusta Bay

The stretch of coast starting about 9km north of Protaras offers some fine cliff-top walks. Access is not entirely obvious. Once on the low escarpments all is straightforward, a bonus being the view of the crumbling suburbs of Famagusta (► 83) – take binoculars.

Karpasia

Much of northern Cyprus is quiet, but the Karpasia peninsula is even quieter, with only the local population going about their business. You should take a map and simply set off on a journey of exploration stopping at any beach, ancient site or village that attracts your attention.

Petounda Point

Take the road west of Kition village (west of Larnaka) towards Petounda Point for about 10km. Keep parallel to the shore until it closes on the road. After another 300–400m it is time to leave the car, find the pebbly shore and have a picnic. It is unlikely that anyone else will be there.

Pomos Point to Kato Pyrgos

This section of coast, northeast of Polis in the west, sees fewer visitors than most others in southern Cyprus, although nothing is guaranteed. Several stretches of dark sand line the various bays and coves. The further east the quieter it is. Here the Troodos Mountains descend dramatically to the sea. In the event of a sudden influx of tourist buses there is the opportunity to retreat quickly into the quiet hills and gaze down on the coast from a good height.

The secluded beaches near Pomos Point face north but are no less sun-kissed for that

Timi Beach

Timi Beach, east of Pafos airport, is not the best of Cyprus's watering places, but the series of sandy coves with the occasional fishing boat have a certain charm. The sea is generally calm and quiet except at weekends when the locals descend upon it from nearby villages.

Cyprus's Famous

Visitors to Cyprus

Few native Cypriots have achieved international celebrity but the island has attracted illustrious visitors throughout its history. Island mythology claims the birth of Aphrodite and visits from a succession of Greek gods. Christian influences were brought by St Paul, St Barnabas and St Lazarus (Lazaros in Greek), and literary visitors have included the French poet Rimbaud and British authors Lawrence Durrell and Colin Thubron. More recently, as a sign of its status as a world troublespot, a succession of international statesmen has been despatched here in attempts to solve the Cyprus Problem.

Makarios

Archbishop Makarios III was the first president of Cyprus. He remains a great Greek Cypriot national hero and statues of him can be seen all around the island.

He was born in 1913 and became a priest at Kykkos Monastery. After a period working in Greece and the United States, he was appointed bishop of Pafos and later archbishop of the whole island. He soon became part of the highly politicised world of the Cypriot Church and its campaign for Enosis, or Union, with Greece and against the British. In 1956, as a result of these activities, he was deported to the Seychelles. A year later he was freed but was not allowed to return to Cyprus. It was from Athens, therefore, that he began the final negotiations for independence, having abandoned Enosis, and in February 1959 a deal was signed. Independence was formally granted in August 1960.

Makarios then became president, but inter-communal strife soon emerged and the United Nations had to keep the peace. Tensions continued to grow and in 1974 Makarios was deposed in a Greek-sponsored military coup led by some remnants of the EOKA movement, who were still campaigning for union with Greece. Makarios escaped, but Turkey invaded and the island was divided, as it remains today. He returned and ruled for another three years before his death in 1977, ushering in a new secular era in Cypriot politics.

Archbishop Makarios, the island's first president and a national hero to Greek Cypriots

Richard the Lion-Heart

King Richard I of England came to Cyprus on his way to the Crusades and changed the course of the island's history. Part of his fleet was shipwrecked in 1191, including the ship carrying his sister and his fiancée, Berengaria. The ruler of Cyprus, Isaac Comnenos, treated them badly and Richard retaliated militarily, having first married Berengaria in St George's Chapel, Limassol. After a month of battles Comnenos surrendered and Richard took control of the whole island. However, he was not much enamoured with his conquest and arranged to pass it on to Guy de Lusignan, a French knight. This ushered in the 300-year Lusignan dynasty.

Top Ten

Above: *Kykkos Monastery*
Right: *Aphrodite of Soli, Cyprus Museum, Nicosia*

15

1
Akamas

✚ 28A2

✉ Cyprus's westernmost peninsula

🍴 Baths of Aphrodite Tourist Pavilion Café (££)

❓ Across the road from the café is a pool under the trees called The Baths of Aphrodite

A beautiful region of hills, valleys and rocky shores, ideal for rambling, with rich and varied flora and diverse wildlife.

This westernmost extremity of Cyprus is unique in the Greek part of the island, not only for its beauty but also for the absence of tourist development. This is explained partly by its remoteness, but more so by the existence of a firing range of the British military – a rich irony.

The vegetation is Mediterranean, with large tracts of impenetrable *maquis* interspersed with a thin covering of pine trees and juniper. Autumn flowering cyclamen is everywhere. In places the landscape is impressively stark with spectacular rock outcrops. On the beaches green and loggerhead turtles still come up to lay their eggs, and occasionally a monk seal may be sighted.

Although there are no metalled roads, the area is becoming popular with motorcyclists and walkers.

Several trails for ramblers have been created, starting by the Baths of Aphrodite, west of Polis. A network of marked paths traverses the hills and information panels outline the types of flora. These are described in a free booklet from the tourist office called *Nature Trails of the Akamas*. The ascent of Mouti tis Sotiras is worth contemplating: it only takes an hour to reach the summit and the view is surely the best in Greek Cyprus. Needless to say, in summer it is a hot and sticky expedition. An alternative is to take a boat from Lakki for a swim and a picnic in one of the delightful coves, perhaps near Fontana Amoroza (Love's Spring), halfway to Cape Arnaoutis.

The magnificent and unspoiled Akamas coast

2

Hala Sultan Tekke &
Larnaka Salt Lake

*A Muslim holy shrine standing on the shore of a
natural landmark, which has very different aspects
in winter and summer.*

 29D2

 3km west of Larnaka on
the Kition road

Jun–Sep, daily 9–7:30;
Oct–May, daily 9–5

The Hala Sultan Tekke's importance is surpassed only by
the shrines of Mecca, Medina and al Aksha (Jerusalem). It
was here that the prophet Mohammed's maternal aunt,
Umm Haram, was buried in
AD 649. Apparently, she fell
from a donkey and broke her
neck whilst participating in an
Arab raid on the island. Three
enormous stones were
raised to mark her grave and
thereafter the site became
an important place of
pilgrimage for Muslims.

The mosque, with its
distinctive dome and
minaret, was built by the
Turks in 1816, though the
tomb was built in 1760.
Visitors can enter the
mosque but must respect
the dress code and remove
their shoes before entering.

In the summer the
surrounding gardens are a
relatively cool haven from the
heat of the Salt Lake. This is
a desert for much of the
year, but in winter the lake
fills with water and attracts a
wide range of migrating
birds. The most spectacular
of the winter visitors are the
flamingos, whose distinctive
pink colour makes an
attractive sight, though their
numbers have greatly
reduced. In summer the water evaporates, leaving a dusty
grey expanse that shimmers in the heat.

The salt was once a significant product in the
island's economy, but today it is no longer economically
viable to collect. It originates from the nearby sea, seeping
up through the porous rocks during the rainy months.

The important Muslim shrine, Hala Sultan Tekke

 Free, but donation
requested

 Bus from Larnaka
centre with drop-off on
the main road

 Kition (Panagia
Angeloktistos) (► 40)

3
Kourion

✚ 28B1

✉ Off the Limassol–Pafos road

☎ 2536 2756

🕐 Jun–Sep, daily 8–7:30; Oct–May, daily 8–5. Note that excavations are in progress on the site and this can mean that some parts are closed at times

✋ Inexpensive

🍴 Café in the tourist pavilion (£)

🚌 From Limassol

↔ Kolossi (► 48), Temple of Apollo Hylates (► 50)

❓ Classical dramas or productions of Shakespeare are performed throughout the summer. The tourist office will have the programme

Kourion is the most important archaeological site in the Greek part of the island, impressively perched on the cliffs overlooking the sea.

There has been some sort of settlement here since 3300 BC, the chalcolithic period, but the first significant town was probably built by Mycenaeans around 1400 BC. It reached the height of its powers under the Romans and it is that influence that is most evident from the ruins. Thereafter it went into decline as it suffered from the attentions of Arab raiders and the population moved inland. Excavations started in 1873 and have continued ever since.

The Theatre presents the most striking image of the whole site. It seated an audience of 3,500 and was probably built by the early Greeks and then extended by the Romans to allow for gladiatorial combat and for man against animal spectacles. It is entirely restored and, in summer, performances of plays and concerts are staged.

The Annexe of Eustolios lies just uphill from the Theatre and has an impressive mosaic floor, which can be observed from raised gangways that run around the courtyard. Further up the hill are the Baths, which also had mosaic floors. The Baths follow the traditional Roman pattern, with the *frigidarium* (cold room), then the *tepidarium* (warm room) and the *caldarium* (hot baths).

Various mechanisms for heating the water, along with furnaces and water tanks, are still in evidence.

At the top of the hill west of the Theatre is the Building of the Achilles Mosaic. Constructed around a courtyard, it has a mosaic showing Achilles in disguise revealing his true identity to Odysseus by mistake. There is also a depiction of Ganymede and the Eagle. The house dates from about AD 4 and was probably a reception area for visitors. A similar house lies a short distance down the track, where the mosaic shows two gladiators in combat. Also visible are the remains of an aqueduct that brought the settlement's water supply to the Fountain House, traces of which can still be seen. Opposite the Fountain House is the Basilica which was built in the 5th century. It has fragments of mosaics on the floor and the roof was once supported by 12 columns, some of which can still be detected.

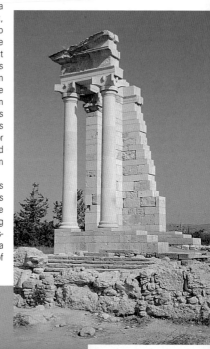

This site covers the main areas of interest, but about 1km towards Pafos off the main road is the Stadium, which once had seating for 6,000. The site is openly accessible and the shape of the arena can be made out, as can some of the seats.

The ancient Greeks chose magnificent sites for their theatres and Kourion's is no exception

4
Kykkos Monastery

✝ 28B2

✉ West of Pedoulas, western Troodos

🕐 Daily

✋ Free; museum inexpensive

🍴 Café nearby (£)

A depiction of the Madonna and Child at Kykkos

The monastery is the largest and richest foundation in Cyprus and is known throughout the Orthodox world.

Kykkos is sited high and alone in the hills of western Cyprus, but even at 1,318m above sea level it is overlooked by higher ground. In summer its cloisters and courtyards are cool; in winter, when the mist descends, the temperature drops alarmingly. Cypriots make pilgrimages to Kykkos from all over southern Cyprus, and hundreds may visit in a weekend. These numbers are swollen by sightseers from the holiday centres.

Kykkos was built about 900 years ago for its icon, the painting of which is attributed to St Luke and was given to a Cypriot monk by Emperor Comnenos for relieving his daughter's sciatica. The present construction with two main cloisters is not of great antiquity – fires destroyed earlier buildings and nothing is older than the 19th century.

In contrast with the spartan conditions of earlier times, today's monks have many modern comforts. Even so, over the years, the community has dwindled from hundreds to a handful and even fewer novices.

The famous icon is called Elousa. It has been encased in silver for 200 years and anyone attempting to gaze directly on it does so under sufferance of horrible punishment. Photography is not permitted. There is also a small one-room museum with items of interest from the monastery's past, mainly religious regalia and books.

In 1926 a novice called Michael Mouskos came to the monastery. He later became Archbishop Makarios III, and president of Cyprus. In those days he would be awake for prayers at 5:30AM followed by a frugal breakfast. During the EOKA campaign the monastery was used by the guerillas for communications and the handling of supplies. Makarios is buried on the hill called Throni, directly above the monastery.

5
Lara

A remote and beautiful area where the land sweeps up to the high hills and turtles come ashore to breed.

Lara is the name of a headland with sandy bays on each side. This splendid coast continues on up to Koppos Island, opposite which the rough road gives out, and then on to the distant northern cape.

The nearest outpost is Ágios Georgios, hardly a village but having a church and harbour and, of course, restaurants. It sees the last of the hard surface road, and from now on the track is terrible, best attempted with an all-terrain vehicle or a motorcycle. And there is quite a lot of it – 8km in all, with one steep area that is a real test of nerve on the cliff edge. Thicket, thorn and mimosa border the road, and only by chance or local knowledge can sandy coves on the rocky shore be found. The beaches of Lara itself are easier to discover, with a sweeping bay to the north and a smaller one to the south.

Lara is now a popular destination for there are regular boat trips from Pafos calling at Ágios Georgios on the way. Such splendid beaches and scenery would attract visitors in any circumstances, but there is a further incentive – Lara's famous turtles. In an attempt to secure the future of these beleaguered and precious amphibians a hatchery has been established at Lara. Paradoxically, this was accompanied by great publicity and many make the trip in the hope of seeing them; in fact there is no certainty of this, much depends on the cycle of the breeding season. An even greater paradox is the proposal to create a holiday resort at Lara by the diocese of Pafos, an intrusion that can only detract from the magnificence of the area.

Looking north to Lara headland and the site of the turtle hatchery

 28A2

 Western Cyprus, north of Pafos

 Café near the headland (£)

6
Mosaics at Pafos

✚ 28A2

✉ A short distance inland from the harbour

☎ 2694 0217

🕐 Jun–Aug, daily 9–7:30; Sep–May, daily 9–5. Closed 1 Jan, 25 Dec, Greek Orthodox Easter Sun

✋ Moderate

🍴 Cafés at the harbour (££)

↔ Saranda Kolones
(► 60), St Paul's Pillar
(► 60), Pafos Fort
(► 59)

Roman houses with impressive and well preserved mosaics depicting colourful scenes from Greek mythology.

The mosaics were found in five large 3rd-century villas that probably belonged to wealthy Roman noblemen. The House of Dionysos was the first to be excavated, after a passing shepherd turned up some fragments of mosaics. The depictions include that of Ganymede being taken to Olympus by an eagle. The most famous mosaic is that of the triumph of Dionysos as he heads across the skies in a chariot drawn by leopards. According to the legend, Dionysos was the first person to discover how to make wine, and his followers are depicted enjoying the fruits of his labour.

The House of Aion displays a fine series of mosaics, which were discovered in 1983. The five scenes starting from the top left show Leda and the Swan; the baby Dionysos; then the middle panel depicts a beauty contest being judged by Aion; on the bottom row is the triumphant procession of Dionysos and the punishment of a musician, Marsyas, who had challenged Apollo to a musical contest and lost. These mosiacs date from the late 4th century.

The House of Orpheus contains representations of Amazon, Hercules and the Lion of Nemea, alongside an impressive

The Roman mosaics display great variety in colour and pattern

mosaic featuring Orpheus surrounded by animals who are listening to his music.

The main mosaic in the House of Theseus is that of Theseus killing the minotaur, although there are some others featuring Achilles and Neptune. The mosaics here are less well preserved than in other areas of the site. A new area – the House of the Four Seasons – was unearthed in 1992. Mosaics showing the Gods of the Seasons and a variety of hunting scenes were found here. As excavations are continuing, parts of these houses may not be open to the public.

7
Nicosia Walled City

Eleven stout bastions superimposed on a circular wall give the city its distinctive and unique plan. Much has survived the centuries.

Nicosia's formidable walls, so masterfully constructed by the Venetians, remain substantially intact, though Pafos Gate to the west is battered and Girne (Kyrenia) Gate's situation ruined. Famagusta Gate has fared better, although it is now a cultural centre, perhaps something of a comedown for what was the important eastern entrance into the city. A lesser but similar indignity has been inflicted on the wide moat (always intended to be dry): this deep and formidable barrier to full-scale attack is now a collection of pleasant gardens, car parks and football pitches. In the end the great walls did not save Nicosia. The Turks broke through in 1570 after a siege of 70 days – a bloody event, with the victors celebrating in an orgy of slaughter.

Today Ledra and Onasagoras streets in the Greek sector are thriving bustling places, and small shops of all kinds are continuously busy. A little to the east the reconstructed buildings known as Laïki Geitonia (➤ 74) are popular with visitors. In the Turkish part of town development moves at a somewhat slower pace.

Along the backstreets there are areas that are conspicuously decrepit. This is not always to be regretted, as low overheads have enabled a Bohemian quarter to grow up around Famagusta Gate, with bars, cafés, a bookshop or two and a small theatre. Close by is a renovated neighbourhood. The buildings, mainly houses, remain substantially as before, but wearing new clothes. Small interesting squares, once rough underfoot, are now smoothly paved.

Of course, Nicosia is the city of the Green Line, a barrier of sandbags and barbed wire that was erected before the young conscripts who now guard it were born.

✛ 28C3

✉ Centre of Nicosia

🍴 Cafés at Laïki Geitonia, Famagusta Gate, Attatürk Square (£)

↔ Nicosia (➤ 70)

Traffic jams streets designed for donkey carts

8
St Hilarion Castle

🕇 28C3

✉ High in the hills west of Kyrenia

🕐 Jun–Sep, daily 9–5; Oct–May, daily 9–1, 2–4:45

✋ Inexpensive

🍴 Café at the gate (£)

↔ Bellapais Abbey (▶ 88)

This fortified former monastery, besieged and taken by Richard the Lion-Heart in 1191, has spectacular coastal views.

Richard the Lion-Heart laid siege to the castle in 1191, and after four days Emperor Isaac Comnenos surrendered. Today the Turkish military controls the heights around the castle, and it is a significant place to advertise their presence.

This is no compact, easily visited site. There are lower, middle and upper wards, with quite a distance between each and a steep climb to the upper section. The big compensation for the effort – fairly substantial in the summer heat – is the unbelievable view. The north shore is directly below and mainland Turkey is plainly visible in the clear air of the cooler months. East and west a spectacular line of peaks and ridges runs into the distance.

St Hilarion, it seems, was a recluse who found refuge on these heights, and built a retreat here. A monastery was established on the site in the 11th century, and was later fortified and then extended by the Lusignans. The lower ward housed the garrison and their horses. A tunnel leads on to the middle ward and a small Byzantine church. Some steps descend to a hall, which may have been a refectory, or banqueting chamber. Adjacent is a belvedere and café. The view over the coast is exceptional.

From a distance the battlements have a fairytale quality, inspiring thoughts of princesses and gallant knights

The path to the upper ward climbs steadily to the mountain top. Even then not everything is accessible, although St John's Tower, in its precipitous location, can be reached by a short detour. The Queen's Window is perhaps the place to stop and rest.

9
Salamis

In legend the founder of Salamis, an impressive archaeological site, was the Greek hero Teucer, brother of Ajax, and son of Telamon.

➕ 29E3

✉ 10km north of Famagusta

🕐 Jun–Sep, daily 9–7; Oct–May, daily 9–1, 2–4:45

✋ Inexpensive

🍴 Café near north entrance (£)

In the 7th century BC Salamis was the first city of Cyprus. It was not until the Roman occupation centuries later that it was succeeded by Pafos in the west. In AD 350 the Byzantines changed the city's name to Constantia and restored its status as the capital. There was much subsequent rebuilding due to earthquakes, but in the 7th century attacks by Arabs left the city in ruins.

In high summer a visit is a memorable occasion, although only the most determined will be able to stay the full course in the great heat. However, the Roman Theatre should not be missed, with its restored tiers of seats rising to an impressive height.

A little further north are the vents and hypocausts of the Baths, opening on to the Gymnasium, all built by the Romans. This structure, its rows of marble columns plainly evident, was damaged by earthquakes and remodelled in Byzantine times, only to collapse later. The columns that we see today were erected as recently as the 1950s.

Columns of the Gymnasium against rare storm clouds

South of the Theatre the huge columns of the granite Forum lie across the site. To the east are the few remains of the church of Ágios Epifanios, built in the 4th century. This northern section of the site was a cultural centre. The Agora is found in the central part, near the Voutra, a 7th-century cistern. Close by are the unimpressive ruins of the Temple of Zeus.

It is a walk of some 500m northeast, towards the sea, to find the Kampanopetra, a large Early Christian basilica, which has been only partially excavated. The Ancient Harbour is about 300m southeast, on the shoreline. Alternatively, cross the main road and walk about 200m to the western site. Here, at the Royal Necropolis, are several important tombs. These were designed for rich citizens, though there are also tombs for ordinary people nearby, called the Cellarka.

10
Troodos Mountains

✝ 28C2

✉ Central Cyprus

🍴 Cafés at Troodos village, Platres, Foini, Kakopetria and other villages (£–££)

Despite their elevation, these are friendly rounded hills with a multitude of charming villages hidden in the pine covered folds.

The Troodos is an extensive area, running from west of Larnaka to the high ground of Mount Olympus, then falling gradually to the western coast. There are many reasons for taking in the delights of the mountains, and they make a refreshing change from the hot beaches and dusty lowlands. Terraced vineyards shape the lower southern slopes, with Aleppo pine covering the higher ground.

Prodromos in springtime, the highest village in Cyprus

Summits may be tree covered or adorned with spiky scrub, relieved occasionally with dried flowers. Northern slopes are different again: dark poplars stand out in the valleys alongside golden oak and rock rose. Summer days are cooler on the high ground and a big attraction in winter is the snow, with skiing on Mount Olympus.

The most impressive of Cyprus's celebrated monasteries are in the Troodos. Chrysorrogiatissa (➤ 62), standing in splendid terrain, is about 45km from Pafos. Kykkos (➤ 20) is more convenient for Limassol, but still half a day's excursion. In the east is Machairas (➤ 80), less splendid, but well worth a visit.

Regrettably few seek out the small Byzantine churches of Panagía tou Araka (➤ 81) and Stavros tou Agiasmati near Lagoudera on the north side of the range. This is understandable, because it is a long drive, but their frescos are extraordinary.

Walks and trails are now popular in Cyprus, and those above Platres (Kaledonia Falls and around Mount Olympus) are detailed in a booklet produced by the tourist office. In western Cyprus the forest takes over, and Cedar Valley (➤ 12) is renowned for its giant timbers. Fortunately for the peace of this marvellous area few people seem prepared to negotiate the difficult roads.

What To See

Above: *chapel alongside Stavrovouni Monastery*
Right: *Nissi Beach sails*

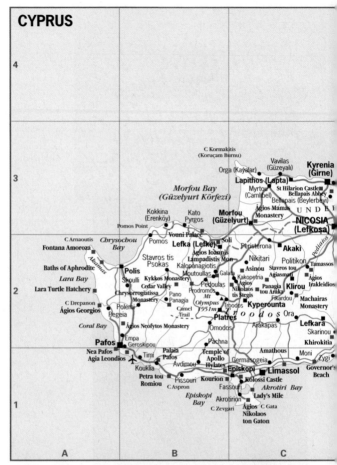

CYPRUS

4

3

C Kormakitis
(Koruçam Burnu)

Orga (Kayalar)

Vavilas
(Güzeyalı)

**Kyrenia
(Girne)**

Lapithos (Lapta)

St Hilarion Castle

Myrtou
(Camlibel)

Bellapais Abbey

*Morfou Bay
(Güzelyurt Körfezi)*

Bellapais (Beylerbeyi)

Kokkina
(Erenköy)

Kato
Pyrgos

**Morfou
(Güzelyurt)**

Ágios Mamas
Monastery

U N D E

**NICOSIA
(Lefkoşa)**

Pomos Point

Vouni Palace

C Arnaoutis

*Chrysochou
Bay*

Pomos

Lefka (Lefke)

Soli

Ágios Ioannis

Peristerona

Akaki

Fontana Amoroza

Stavros tis
Psokas

Lampadistis Mon.

Nikitari

Politikon

Kalopanagiotis

Asinou

Stavros tou
Agiasmati

Tamassos

Polis

Moutoullas

Kakopetria

Baths of Aphrodite

Skoulli

Kykkos Monastery

Cedar Valley

Pedoulas

Galata

**Ágios
Irakleidios**

Lara Bay

Chrysorrogiatissa
Monastery

Prodromos

Ágios
Nikolaos
tis Stegis

Panagia
tou Araka

Klirou

Lara Turtle Hatchery

Pano
Panagia

*Mt
Olympus
1951m*

Trôodos

Fikardou

**Machairas
Monastery**

C Drepanon

Polemi

Camel
Trail

Kyperounta

Ora

Ágios Georgios

Pegeia

Platres

T r o o d o s

Lefkara

Coral Bay

Ágios Neofytos Monastery

Omodos

Arakapas

Skarinou

Empa

Pachna

Khirokitia

Pafos

Geroskipou

Nea Pafos

Timi

**Palaia
Pafos**

Temple of
Apollo
Hylate

Amathous

Moni

Germasogeia

Agia Leondios

Kouklia

Avdimou

Episkopi

Limassol

*Governor's
Beach*

Zygi

Petra tou
Romiou

Pissouri

Kourion

Kolossi Castle

C Aspron

Fassouri

Akrotiri Bay

*Episkopi
Bay*

Akrotirion

Lady's Mile

C Zevgari

Ágios
Nikolaos
ton Gaton

C Gata

2

1

A   B   C

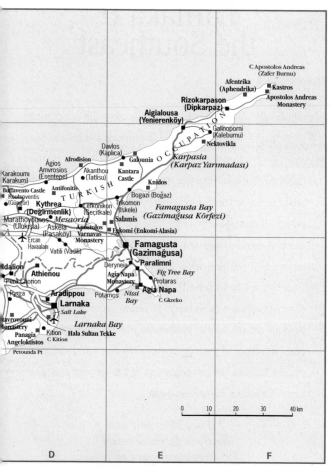

C Apostolos Andreas
(Zafer Burnu)

Afentrika
(Aphendrika)
Kastros
Apostolos Andreas
Monastery

Rizokarpason
(Dipkarpaz)

Aigialousa
(Yenierenköy)
Galinoporni
(Kaleburnu)
Nektovikla

Davlos
(Kaplıca)
Galounia

Afrodision
Akanthou
(Tatlısu)
Kantara
Castle
Knidos

Ágios
Amvrosios
(Esentepe)

Karakoumi
(Karakum)
Antifonitis

Buffavento Castle
Koutsoventis
(Güngör)

Kythrea
(Değirmenlik)
Lefkonikon
(Geçitkale)
Trikomon
(İskele)

Marathovounos
(Ulukışla)
Mesaoria
Salamis
Famagusta Bay
(Gazimağusa Körfezi)

Askela
(Pasaköy)
Apostolos
Varnavas
Monastery
Enkomi (Enkomi-Alasia)

Ercan
Havaalanı
Vatili (Vadili)
Famagusta
(Gazimağusa)
Paralimni

Idalion
Athienou
Deryneia
Agia Napa
Monastery
Fig Tree Bay
Protaras

Pera Chorion
Potamos
Agia Napa

Pyrga
Aradippou
Nissi
Bay
C Gkreko

Larnaka
Salt Lake

Stavrovouni
Monastery
Larnaka Bay

Panagia
Angeloktistos
Kition
Hala Sultan Tekke
C Kition

Petounda Pt

Bogazi (Boğaz)

Karpasia
(Karpaz Yarımadası)

OCCUPATION

TURKISH

0 10 20 30 40 km

| D | E | F |

Looking west along the rocky shore from Cape Gkreko

29

Larnaka &
the Southeast

This part of Cyprus was once the agricultural heartland and it still provides the bulk of the Cypriot potato crop, which thrives in the distinctive red soil. However, in the last 20 years the agricultural industry has been supplanted by tourism, focused on two, previously quiet, resorts – Agía Napa and Protaras. The growth of these areas has been dramatic – in 1974 Agía Napa provided tourists with 126 beds, today that figure is 14,000.

Beaches are the main attraction of this region, and the coastline offers a good range of places worth stopping at, although crowds tend to descend on summer weekends. The other attractions of the area are more low key: some traditional villages, Larnaka, the only settlement of any size, and a glimpse of the 'forbidden city' of Famagusta.

> *'If you blew your nose loudly in Larnaca before driving at speed to Limassol you would almost certainly meet someone on arrival who had already heard of the fact.'*
>
> LAWRENCE DURRELL
> *Bitter Lemons* (1957)

Larnaka

Larnaka is a significant tourist and commercial centre and is a convenient base for exploring the island, though its own places of interest are fairly limited. The modern city is built on the remains of ancient Kition, which was, according to the legend, established by one of Noah's grandsons in the 13th century BC. Out of this settlement Larnaka became an important trading centre, from where the island's main export of copper was shipped, and it has long had a large foreign population.

The town can be very busy at rush hour and the narrow streets and one-way system do not help the foreign driver. Visitors should try to park quickly and explore on foot. The pedestrianised seafront is lined with cafés and at the northern end of the promenade is a large marina with berths for 450 yachts. Larnaka is the main yachting centre of the island and the port facilities here attract boats from all over the eastern Mediterranean. There is a very popular beach by the centre of town, but it is man-made and is certainly not among the best on the island. The seafront road provides amenities for the captive tourist with an abundance of cafés, restaurants and ice-cream sellers.

Larnaka has a long history, but much of the evidence of that history has been covered by the sprawl of the modern city. However the enthusiastic will be able to track down archaeological remains and historic churches.

Relax on Larnaka's town beach

31

What to See in Larnaka

ÁGIOS LAZAROS CHURCH

Legend states that St Lazarus, having been raised from the dead by Christ, came to Larnaka to live out the rest of his days and when he definitely died he was buried here. His remains, however, were stolen and only his empty tomb is visible in the south apse. The church itself was built in the 9th century and extensively restored in the 17th century, including the decoration of its extremely ornate interior.

🕆 32B1
✉ Agiou Lazarou Street
🕑 Apr–Aug, Mon–Sat
8–12:30, 3:30–6:30;
Sep–Mar, Mon–Sat
8–12:30, 2:30–5.
Still used as a church
🚫 Free
🍴 Cafés nearby (££)

ARCHAEOLOGICAL MUSEUM

This museum has a good collection of exhibits, some of which date back as far as 3000 BC, from the local sites of Kition and Choirokoitia. The first room contains statues and terracotta figurines. The second room houses the pottery collection, along with some Mycenaean vases. Other rooms contain neolithic artefacts, including a reconstruction of a neolithic tomb, and finally some Roman glassware. The museum's pleasant garden contains a large number of fragments of statues and a circular mosaic pavement.

🕆 32B2
✉ Kalograion Street
☎ 2463 0169
🕑 Mon–Wed, Fri 9–2:30,
Thu 9–2:30, 3–5. Closed
1 Jan, afternoons
Jul–Aug, 25 Dec
🚫 Inexpensive
🍴 Cafés nearby (£)

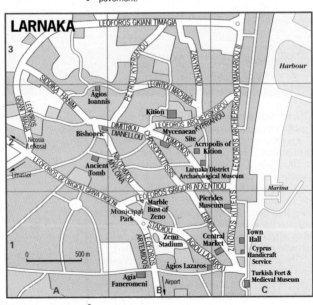

KITION ✪✪

The remains of the ancient city can be found at a number of sites. The most visible ruins are on Leontiou Machaira near the Archaeological Museum. The ditches and walls date from the 12th and 13th centuries BC, when they enclosed the city. It is also possible to make out the traces of a Phoenician temple, and the sharp eyed may detect images of ships carved into the south wall.

➕ 32B2
✉ Leontiou Machaira Street
🕐 Mon–Wed, Fri 9–2:30, Thu 9–2:30, 3–5. Closed afternoons Jul–Aug, 1 Jan and 25 Dec
💷 Inexpensive

The main site at Kition – much of its stone was shipped to Egypt to build the Suez Canal

PIERIDES MUSEUM ✪✪

This museum was founded in 1974 to house the private collection of antiquities of Demetrius Pierides, covering the neolithic to the Middle Ages. The collection, of 3,600 exhibits, is housed in the Pierides family's fine 19th-century house, and contains early pottery decorated with various designs, artefacts from the site at Marion, mainly jugs and vases, and one of the most important collections of Roman glassware and jewellery in Europe. The main hall has some early maps of Cyprus and traditional folk artefacts.

➕ 32C1
✉ Zinonos Kitieos Street
☎ 2465 8848
🕐 Tue–Fri 10–1, 5–8. Sat 10–1. Closed 1 Jan, 25 Dec, Greek Orthodox Easter Sun
💷 Moderate
🍴 Cafés nearby (£)

TURKISH FORT AND MEDIEVAL MUSEUM ✪

The fort was built in 1625 by the Turks to defend the city against raiders but was soon adapted for use as a prison. It now contains a small medieval museum, featuring mainly suits of armour. There are also some artefacts from Kition and other excavations in the area. In summer theatrical performances sometimes take place in the courtyard.

➕ 32C1
✉ Larnaka seafront, south end of Ankara Street
🕐 Jun–Aug, Mon–Fri 9–7:30; Sep–May, Mon–Fri 9–5. Closed 1 Jan, 25 Dec
💷 Inexpensive
🍴 Cafés nearby (££)

Did you know ?

Zeno, the founder of the Stoic philosophy was born here. However, he spent most of his life teaching in Athens, where he lived to the extraordinary age of 98. He died, not of old age, but by committing suicide, presumably unable to be stoical any longer.

A Walk Around Larnaka

Distance
2km

Time
1–2 hours

Start/end point
The Marina
➕ 32C2
🚌 18

Lunch
Old Mansion Archontiko (£)
✉️ 24 Athinon Avenue
☎️ 2465 5905

The walk starts at the northern end of the seafront by the marina.

Head inland on Pavlou Street, passing the tourist office before turning left into Zinonos Kitieos Street.

This is the main shopping street of Larnaka. It also contains the Pierides Museum, which houses an enormous range of ancient and historical artefacts from all over Cyprus (➤ 33).

Pass the yellow building of the Armenian Church and later the municipal market at the corner of Ermou Street. There is a confusing maze of intersections at the end of Zinonos Kitieos Street requiring a sharp right and then follow the road round to the left.

The old mosque, which is passed, is now a youth hostel in the Laiki Geitonia. A little further (about five minutes) is Ágios Lazaros church (➤ 32).

After exploring the church and its graveyard, head back towards the seafront down Agiou Lazarou Street.

This was once the Turkish part of town and the minaret of Djami Kebir mosque can be seen. Although it is still used by visiting Muslims, it is open to the public when services are not taking place.

Follow the main road back to the shore, and Larnaka fort is to the right (➤ 33).

It is worth pausing for a moment to take in the view from the south of the fort, where the coastline stretches away in a long strip of tourist development.

It is a straight walk along the seafront, or along the beach, back to the marina.

The campanile of Ágios Lazaros Church

What to See in the Southeast

AGÍA NAPA ✪✪

Agía Napa is a major tourist resort but the centre of the village retains some charm by virtue of its **monastery** and its well-watered gardens, which present a welcome haven from the bustle outside.

The monastic church was built in the 16th century over a cave in which an icon of the Virgin Mary was supposedly found. In the 17th century the monastery became very rich, owning much of the land in the area. It fell into disrepair during the 18th century and was abandoned, but was later restored under British rule and now belongs to the World Council of Churches.

The **Marine Life Museum** was opened in 1992 to display the marine life of Cyprus. The exhibits include a large number of fossils, some dating back to 220 million years ago. There is also an extensive collection of shells found in local waters, as well as sea urchins, starfish and corals. Exhibits relating to the sea turtles for which Cyprus is famous can also be found. Photographs and specimens of contemporary sea life conclude the exhibition.

✚ 29E2
Monastery
✉ Centre of Agía Napa village
🕐 Daily
💷 Free
🍴 Many cafés nearby (££)
Marine Life Museum
✉ 25 Agias Mavris Street
☎ 2372 3409
🕐 Mon–Wed, Fri, Sat 9–2; Thu 9–2, 3–6
💷 Inexpensive
🍴 Many cafés nearby (££)

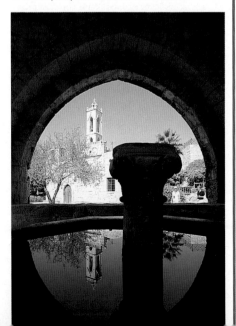

The still waters of the fountain within the monastery are a sharp contrast to the frenetic activity outside

A Drive Around Cape Gkreko

Distance
135km

Time
3–5 hours

Start/end point
Larnaka town centre
 32B2

Lunch
Harbour fish restaurants (££)
✉ Agía Napa

This drive runs northeast from Larnaka town centre, following the main road to the British base of Dhekalia.

Turn right into the base, passing through checkpoints at either end. At the other side of the base the road returns to the coastline.

There are a number of good beaches along this road, as well as the village of Zylofagou. Close by is Potamos creek (➤ 40), a delightful little fishing harbour with a safe – and usually quiet – beach.

The main road leads directly into Agía Napa, or there is an older, quieter route that runs closer to the coast – turn right off the main road, and then left to pass the beaches of Makronisos, Nissi and Sandy Bay (➤ 40).

Agía Napa harbour lies 1km east of Nissi. Another good sandy beach stretches away from the harbour out to the headland, where the cliffs have been carved by the water into spectacular formations. Agía Napa, the most popular destination in this area (➤ 35), lies just uphill. The many attractions here include a splendid marine life museum , a Luna Park, Skycoasters and Waterworld, an exciting water-based theme park (➤ 108). More sedate visitors can go instead to the ancient monastery in the village.

The route continues east on the Paralimni road. Once outside Agía Napa, turn off to follow signs to Cape Gkreko.

There are good views from the cape and from the main road that leads to Protaras (Fig Tree Bay; ➤ 41). Beyond Protaras there are numerous small coves, which offer pleasant, safe swimming.

Turn left through Paralimni and then complete the round trip by heading back towards Sotira, Liopetri and Zylofagou, where the road rejoins the main route to Larnaka.

The fine white sand of Nissi Beach is lapped by a clear, turquoise sea

Food & Drink

Cyprus has plenty of fresh produce and meat and visitors should take the opportunity to make the most of the fruits that are so plentiful in the summer months. Quite apart from the well-known crops of citrus fruits, there are peaches, plums, cherries, the ubiquitous melon and bananas – all easily available in season. Water melons, in particular, are sold from roadside stalls.

Cypriot wine suits most palates, but zivania *and* ouzo *are potent distillations to be treated with caution*

Greek Cuisine

The old staples of Greek cuisine, moussaka, *stifado*, kebab and Greek salad will be much in evidence. The *meze* is perhaps a good way to get an insight into Cypriot food. *Meze*, or *mezedhes*, is a series of small different dishes that are provided throughout an evening, and may cover absolutely everything or pursue a fish or a meat theme. In a good restaurant the *meze* can contain up to 30 different dishes and it is important to pace yourself through the meal.

Kebab (*souvlaki*) appears on all menus and lamb is another common dish on offer, either lamb chops or the more traditional *kleftiko*, which consists of large pieces of lamb baked slowly in traditional *kleftiko* ovens. Cypriots also have a taste for smoked meats, with the traditional *loukanika* sausage a favourite.

Fish is expensive, although *kalamari* – squid cooked in batter – is good value and widely available. Other fish options include swordfish, red mullet (*barbouni* in Greek), whitebait and sea bass. Alternatively, fresh trout is on the menu in some of the mountain villages.

Halloumi cheese is the main dairy product distinctive to the island. It is made from goat's milk and is often served

grilled. It is the food that the many expatriate Cypriots living in Britain claim they miss the most.

Visitors should seek out some of the cake shops that attract local custom. The traditional Greek desserts such as *baklava* and *cadefi* may be too sweet for some tastes but the wide range of custard-based cakes should appeal to all, as will the biscuits, which can be bought by weight in these shops.

A similar range of food is available in the Turkish part of the island. Some dishes such as *sis kebab* and *cacik* (cucumber and yoghurt salad) will already be familiar, but there are many other delights, among them *elma dizmesi*, a dish of apples and meat patties, and *cuvecte yaz turlusu*, a tasty summer stew.

Island produce for sale outside Kykkos Monastery includes soujoukko for those with a sweet tooth

Wine, Brandy and Beer

Cypriot wine is plentiful and inexpensive, and it is claimed that it has been made in Cyprus since 2000 BC. The main wineries are at Limassol, but, increasingly, smaller producers are developing and some of the villages and monasteries now produce their own wines. It is an important business with 23 million litres a year exported to the United Kingdom alone.

Commandaria sweet wine is one of Cyprus's best known wines and it is claimed that it was drunk during the old festivals of Aphrodite. However, its origins can only be definitively traced back to the estate of the Knights Hospitaller at Kolossi, 700 years ago.

The island also produces brandy, and brandy sour is a popular tourist drink; it combines the local brandy with lemons and angostura bitters. Keo and Carlsberg beers are made locally and provide an alternative to the wines.

Labels reflecting the wine's origins at the estate of the Knights Hospitaller

39

DERYNEIA

This village gives an insight into recent Cypriot history. It is the nearest settlement to Famagusta and one villager has set up a viewing point where tourists, for a small fee, can climb up to the roof of his house and look through a telescope across no man's land to the closed city of Famagusta. Deryneia is also the place where trouble flared up in 1996 and two Greek Cypriots were killed while approaching the Turkish military zone.

29E2
✉ 11km north of Agía Napa
🍴 Café in village (£), restaurant on road to Paralimni (££)
🚌 From Protaras, in summer every hour 8–3, Sun last bus 1:30

HALA SULTAN TEKKE AND SALT LAKE (► 17, TOP TEN)

> ## Did you know?
>
> *Some 256sq km of Cyprus is British territory, contained within the three main military bases at Dhekalia, Akrotiri and Episkopi. These areas are subject to British law and are officially known as Sovereign Base Areas.*

NISSI BEACH

Nissi Beach is where tourist development in this area started. It is a pleasant sandy beach, though it can be very crowded in summer, with a rocky island just offshore. The presence of a sand bar makes it possible to wade to the island, an adventure that appeals especially to children. Those going to the island should, however, bear in mind that it is made up of rough and spiky rocks and suitable footwear is necessary.

29E2
✉ 2km west of Agía Napa
🍴 Several cafés (£)

PANAGÍA ANGELOKTISTOS CHURCH (KITION CHURCH)

Panagía Angeloktistos, which means 'built by angels', was constructed in the 11th century on the remains of a 5th-century church. It has many ornate icons but its main attraction is a mosaic that depicts angels attending the Virgin Mary as she holds Christ; it is a very intricate composition, of a style not found elsewhere in Cyprus. The mosaic will be lit up for visitors on request.

29D2
✉ Edge of the village on road to Mazotos
☎ 2442 2626
🕐 Daily 9–5. If locked ask for the key at the nearby café
💷 Donation requested
🍴 Café nearby (£)
🚌 From Larnaka

POTAMOS

This pleasant creek serves as a small fishing harbour. At the shoreline there is a café and a long, if slightly rocky, beach with the church of Ágios Georgios at its western

29E2
✉ 14km west of Agía Napa
🍴 Café on beach (£)

end. Early in the morning, when the fishermen are returning with their catch, it is a lovely place. The beach is usually quiet and provides an opportunity for calm, safe swimming.

PROTARAS
★★

Protaras, also known as Fig Tree Bay because of a fig tree that was once its only landmark, is a fully fledged resort full of hotels, restaurants and the ubiquitous discos. The beach is sandy and there are very good watersports facilities. The offshore rocky islet offers the chance of some small degree of seclusion although you have to be a fairly strong swimmer to reach it.

STAVROVOUNI
★★

The monastery of Stavrovouni is set at a height of 690m and the views from the top of the hill are spectacular. There has been a religious community here since AD 327 when St Helena brought a fragment of the True Cross from Jerusalem. It is claimed that the piece is still in the monastery, covered by a silver casing. The original buildings were destroyed by Arab and Turkish raiders and those visible today date mainly from the 17th century. They are still occupied by a devout community of monks and women are not allowed inside.

29E2

✉ 8km north of Cape Gkreko on east coast

🍴 Numerous cafés and restaurants (£–££)

🚌 From Agia Napa in summer: every hour 9–5, Sun 10–5

29D2

✉ 40 km west of Larnaka

🕐 Men only. Apr–Aug, daily 8–12, 3–6; Sep–Mar, daily 8–12, 2–5

🎟 Free

The chapel at Stavrovouni, with the barren landscape of Larnaka district beyond

Limassol &
the South

This region has something for all tastes and all interests: an attractive coastline, a medieval castle, spectacular views, archaeological remains and, for the mythologically inclined, the birthplace of Aphrodite. Those with an interest in history will find plenty to occupy them. The 9,000 year-old site at Khirokitia is the oldest settlement on the island while Kourion and its restored amphitheatre has relics from the Mycenaean, Persian and Roman periods. There are links with ancient mythology too, a temple to Apollo and Petra tou Romiou, the place where Aphrodite is supposed to have emerged from the foaming sea. A newer tradition, only 500 years old, is found in the lacemaking village of Lefkara, and beyond Limassol are the vital ingredients for any Cypriot holiday, some good beaches.

' They say Limassol is as large again as it was before the occupation and certainly it gives one the impression of being almost a new town. Houses are springing up everywhere, almost by magic. '

ANONYMOUS
BRITISH ARMY OFFICER
stationed in Cyprus in 1882

Limassol

Limassol's main claim to fame is that England's Richard the Lion-Heart was shipwrecked here and married his fiancée Berengaria in the town. The Knights Hospitaller developed Limassol as a trading post based on export of the Commandaria wine, which they made from the vineyards surrounding Kolossi. However, it was only in the 19th century that its major asset, the deep-water port, began to be appreciated and the town became a significant commercial centre.

In recent years Limassol has seen massive tourist development and there is a line of hotels along each approach road. It is a modern town – new building and road works proliferate – but it does not lack atmosphere and offers good shopping, nightlife and restaurants. The carnival in spring and the wine festival in early September are particularly lively times to visit the town.

The sights of Limassol are easily explored on foot, indeed those coming by car should be prepared for traffic problems and a fiendishly complicated one-way system. The main historical sight is the castle and medieval museum. There are also a couple of mosques, with distinctive minarets, serving as reminders of a time when Limassol had a Turkish quarter. The main shopping area is around Agiou Andreou Street.

Agiou Andreou Street, once bustling with traffic, now a pedestrianised shopping haven

What to See in Limassol

 28C1
 8km east of Limassol
Jun–Aug, daily 9–7:30;
Sep–May, daily 9–5
Inexpensive
From Limassol and
Larnaka

*Ancient pavements and
pillars of the Agora,
Amathous*

AMATHOUS

The archaeological remains of Amathous are spread over a wide area and include a rock-cut tomb in the grounds of the Amathus Beach Hotel.

The most easily accessible ruins are of the Agora, in a fenced site just off the main road on the inland side. This was the market area and though it is a relatively small site there are many pillars still visible, which make it quite an impressive place. Up a track from the Agora is the Acropolis and remains of a Temple to Aphrodite. There is evidence that some of the site lies underwater, which offers exciting opportunities for snorkellers and scuba-divers to explore.

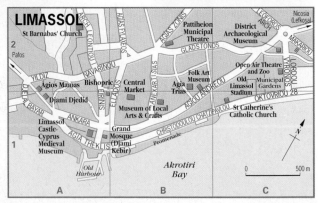

CASTLE AND CYPRUS MEDIEVAL MUSEUM ✪✪

The main buildings of the castle were constructed in the 14th century on the site of an earlier Byzantine fortification. The chapel in which Richard the Lion-Heart and Berengaria were married was part of the original castle but is no longer standing. The castle was occupied by the Turks and later by the British as an army headquarters.

The Cyprus Medieval Museum is now housed here. The basement contains replicas of sculptures and photographs of the Byzantine churches of Cyprus. Upstairs the exhibits are found in small rooms off a central hall with the most memorable items – armour and weapons – on the second floor. The final flight of stairs leads out on to the battlements where there are good views of the city. The most distinctive sights on the skyline are the two mosques, Djami Djedid and Djami Kebir, reminders that this was once the Turkish part of town.

✚ 44A1
✉ Eirinis Street, near the old·harbour
☎ 2533 0419
🕐 Mon–Sat 9–5, Sun 10–1. Closed 1 Jan, 25 Dec
👜 Inexpensive
🍴 Many cafés nearby (£)

DISTRICT ARCHAEOLOGICAL MUSEUM ✪

The garden contains a sundial that supposedly belonged to the British Lord Kitchener. Inside, Room 1 contains neolithic tools and pottery from Amathous and Kourion. These artefacts are very old with some dating back to 2300 BC. Room 2 has later figurines and Roman coins. The final room contains statues from Amathous including those of Artemis and the Egyptian god Bes.

Below: *the Gardens are a cool oasis*

✚ 44C2
✉ Kanningos and Vyronos Street
☎ 2530 5157
🕐 Mon–Sat 9–5, Sun 10–1. Closed 1 Jan, 25 Dec, Greek Orthodox Easter Sun)
👜 Inexpensive

MUNICIPAL GARDENS AND ZOO ✪✪

The Municipal Gardens offer some welcome greenery in a dusty city. They also contain a small zoo, though the animals are kept in poor conditions. There is a small open-air theatre, where productions are held during the summer. The Gardens are also the site of the annual Limassol Wine Festival, held in September. All the local wine companies set up stalls and offer an evening of free wine tasting accompanied by music and dancing.

✚ 44C2
✉ 28 Oktovriou Street
☎ 2558 8345
🕐 Gardens: daylight hours. Zoo: daily 9–7
👜 Gardens: free. Zoo: moderate
🍴 Café in the Gardens (£)

A Limassol Walk

Distance:
2.5km

Time:
1–3½ hours

Start point
Seafront car park
➕ 44B1

End point
Municipal Gardens
➕ 44C1

Lunch
Many cafés opposite the castle (£)
🗷 Eirinis Street

This walk starts on the seafront by the car park. The promenade is followed southwest to reach a small roundabout which marks the old harbour, complete with fishing boats. There is a small reptile house on one corner with a collection of local and foreign species.

Proceed inland to the 14th-century castle and Cyprus Medieval Museum (➤ 45). Turn right along Genthliou Mitella Street and pass a mosque that is still in use.

This was once the Turkish part of the town and many of the older houses are of a typical Turkish design. The municipal fruit and vegetable market lies just east of the mosque.

Continue generally northeast until the road leads into Agiou Andreou Street, the main shopping street (➤ 106).

> ### Did you know ?
>
> *It is claimed that wine has been made in Cyprus for 4,000 years. There are four wineries in Limassol run by Keo, Etko, Loel and Sodap. The wine with longest history is Commandaria which Richard the Lion-Heart called 'the wine of kings and the king of wines'.*

There are many narrow alleyways in this area and they are interesting to explore, though walkers should not worry about getting lost as they will eventually emerge on to the wider thoroughfare. Agiou Andreou has a wide range of shops, with goods ranging from the usual souvenirs to leather goods and jewellery.

After about 1km Agía Trias Church can be visited a short way up Agias Triados Street, just before Zinonos Street. Returning to the main road the Folk Art Museum is found a little way on to the left. One kilometre further along Agiou Andreou Street, at the north side of the Municipal Gardens, turn right on Kanningkos Street to reach the Archaeological Museum (➤ 45), 200m to the left. The walk ends in the Municipal Gardens, which offer peace after the busy city streets.

What to See in the South

AKROTIRI PENINSULA

The area contains a good beach, a salt lake and a historic church. In summer the salt lake has a distinctive grey colour and you can smell the salt; in winter it fills with water and is a stopping off point for passing flamingos. Lady's Mile Beach is sandy and offers safe swimming in shallow sea. The far end is closed off, marking the start of the British base at Akrotiri – the occasional military jet may disturb the peace.

The monastery of Ágios Nikolaos ton Gaton (St Nicholas of the Cats) is reached on a track at the southern end of the beach. It was founded in AD 325, though the buildings seen today were constructed in the 13th century and have been restored since. The cats in the name are still much in evidence.

🔲 28C1

Ágios Nikolaos ton Gaton
🕐 Daily. Closed during siesta
🎫 Free
🍴 Cafés on beach (£)

AVDIMOU BEACH

Avdimou Beach is a good long sandy stretch, though the water becomes deep very quickly. There is a small taverna at its eastern end and it is usually quiet, but at weekends it can be busy with service personnel and their families. It is part of the British Sovereign Base and so has not seen any tourist development.

🔲 28B1
✉ 3km off main road, opposite turning to Avdimou village
🍴 Taverna on beach (£)

GOVERNOR'S BEACH

The beach is reached by steps cut out of the steep white cliffs. The astonishingly dark sand is its most distinctive feature and can get painfully hot by the middle of a summer's day. The beach, although narrow, is popular with local people and can be very busy on summer weekends.

🔲 28C1
✉ Junction 16 Nicosia–Limassol motorway
🍴 Cafés on clifftop (£)

Governor's Beach – dark sands and white cliffs

➕ 28C2
✉ Off Junction 14
Nicosia–Limassol
motorway
☎ 2432 2710
🕐 Jun–Aug, daily 9–7:30;
Sep–May, daily 9–5.
Closed 1 Jan, 25 Dec,
Greek Orthodox
Easter Sun
💷 Inexpensive

The imposing Kolossi Castle

➕ 28C1
✉ 14.5km from Limassol
town centre
🕐 Jun–Aug, daily 9–7:30;
Sep–May, daily 9–5.
Closed 1 Jan, 25 Dec,
Greek Orthodox
Easter Sun
💷 Cheap
🍴 Café on site (£)
🚌 From Limassol

KHIROKITIA (CHOIROKOITIA) ✪

This is the oldest archaeological site on the island, dating from 6800 BC when it was home to 2,000 people who farmed the surrounding land.

The most distinctive feature of the settlement is the beehive-shape houses, which come in two sizes, one about 4m across and the other 8m. They were built close together and linked by narrow passageways, and it was apparently a crowded settlement. The inhabitants tended to bury their dead under the floor of the house and then build on top, and some houses have revealed up to eight different periods of occupation.

The settlement is best explored by following the vestiges of the main street, with House A near the entrance being the easiest to make out. A second group of ruins has the remains of pillars visible which once supported the roof. From there the site becomes more complicated and the best views are from the top of the hill from where the wider perspective can reveal its layout.

KOLOSSI CASTLE ✪✪✪

Kolossi was the headquarters of the Knights Hospitaller, who probably built the first castle in the late 13th century. They exploited the fertile land in the area, using locally produced sugar and grapes to make Commandaria wine.

The castle suffered from a number of attacks by Egyptian Mameluke raiders in the 14th century, and the buildings visible today date from a rebuilding that took place in the 15th century. The Turks took it over in 1570 and sugar production continued until 1799.

Visitors pass over a drawbridge into a pleasant garden and then into the keep, which has walls 2.75m thick and is three storeys (23m) high. The defenders might have poured boiling liquids from the machicoulis on to any attackers below.

Much of the ground floor was used as a storage area. The first floor has two large rooms and a kitchen. On the top floor were the apartments of the Grand Commander, which have a spacious, airy feel to them from four large windows. A spiral staircase leads onto the roof, from where there are good views. The large vaulted building in the grounds was the place where the sugar was made.

KOURION (► 18–19, TOP TEN)

LEFKARA ✪✪

The village is divided into two halves, Pano (upper) and Kato (lower) Lefkara, and is a very popular tourist destination. Visitors who prefer to avoid the crowds come in the early morning.

Lefkara is known for its lace, called *lefkaritika*; it first became famous in 1481 when Leonardo da Vinci ordered some for Milan Cathedral. The lace then became popular with local Venetian ladies and the lacemaking industry took off. The tradition continues to flourish and rather ferocious ladies will offer their wares vigorously to passing tourists. Those wishing to buy should take care to ensure that it is the genuine article and not imported. There are also a number of silverware shops.

The main street of Pano Lefkara is now designed to cater for tourists but the narrow alleys to either side are still peaceful places to wander. There is also a small **museum** of lacemaking and silverware, signposted uphill from the main street.

🔲 28C2
✉ 9km northwest of junction 13 of the Nicosia–Limassol motorway
🍴 Cafés in the main street of the upper village (£)
Museum
☎ 2434 2326
🕐 Mon–Thu 9:30–4, Fri–Sat 10–4
♿ Inexpensive

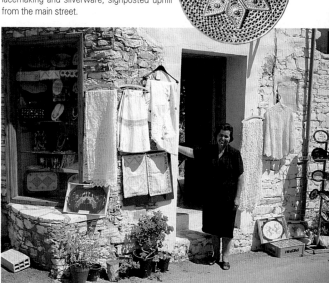

The lower half of the village is often neglected but is worth a visit. Its church of Archangel Michael has some beautiful 18th-century icons and there are good views across the hills from outside the building. The distinctive houses in this part of the village are painted blue and white and its streets are extremely narrow and therefore traffic free.

Above: *a local lady patiently awaits the first trade of the day*
Inset: *intricate silver filigree pendant*

49

➕ 28B1
✉ 24km east of Pafos
🍴 Two cafés, one in tourist pavilion (£)

Petra tou Romiou, the legendary birthplace of Aphrodite

➕ 28B1
✉ Limassol–Pafos road
🕐 Jun–Aug, daily 9–7:30;
Sep–May, daily 9–5.
Closed 1 Jan, 25 Dec,
Greek Orthodox
Easter Sun
✋ Inexpensive

PETRA TOU ROMIOU ✪✪✪

This is one of the most photographed sites on the whole island. The name means the Rock of Romios and the two large rocks in the sea, set against the white cliffs, provide a spectacular scene. There are two official places to stop – one close to the rock, just back from the shore, where there is a café and a car park, the other higher up in the cliffs, where there is a tourist pavilion. However, the best view, coming from Limassol, is on the final bend before the road starts to descend; some scrubland on the left makes a convenient stopping place.

Legend states that this was the birthplace of Aphrodite, where she emerged from the foaming water. The beach itself is rather shingly, and it is not ideal for swimming because it gets rough around the rocks, but it is worth stopping to soak up the mysterious atmosphere.

TEMPLE OF APOLLO HYLATES ✪✪

The temple was first used as a place of devotion in the 8th century BC, though the present ruins date from AD 100, when it was rebuilt after an earthquake. There is a waymarked path and map to guide the visitor around the site. The circular remains of a votive pit are worth a closer look. The pit was used to store unwanted ritual gifts and archaeologists have found it a rich source of artefacts. The path then leads to the Temple of Apollo, which has been partially restored, its high columns a striking reminder of ancient times.

A shed structure covers the Priest's House, and though you have to peer through the fence you can see some mosaics and pillars.

The remaining buildings of interest are the Palaestra, which was an open space used for sporting activities, and a nearby complex of baths.

A Drive from Limassol to Petra tou Romiou

The drive begins in Limassol town centre.

Head towards the new port, then turn west to Asomatos and Fassouri, passing through citrus groves.

The dense groves around the village provide a pleasant drive, and guided tours are also available.

Turn north to Kolossi Castle, a seat of the Knights Hospitaller (▶ 48). After Kolossi village, turn left and in 2km the road passes through the village of Episkopi.

This village was founded in the 7th century by refugees from Kourion. More recently it has become home to British services personnel and their families from the nearby British base. From the village it is a short detour to Kourion (▶ 18), the most impressive archaeological site in the south of the island.

Rejoin the main road, taking extreme care on the dangerous bends, and continue towards Pafos.

In about 1km, on the inland side of the road, is Kourion Stadium and after a further 2km is the Temple of Apollo Hylates, another very impressive ancient site (▶ 50). Immediately beyond this, the road enters the British base of Episkopi to start a steep descent to the green playing fields of Happy Valley. These are a striking contrast to their dusty surroundings.

To the west of the base is a turning to Avdimou Beach (▶ 47), opposite the turning to Avdimou village, lying 3km away by a very narrow track. The main route continues along the coast.

Pissouri, a few kilometres further, provides an alternative beach and the possibility of lunch in the village. Beyond here the road runs high in the cliffs, with spectacular scenery, but on a slow road.

Continue for another 6km to reach Petra tou Romiou, the legendary birthplace of Aphrodite (▶ 50).

Distance
65km

Time
1½–5 hours

Start point
Limassol town centre
➕ 28C1

End point
Petra tou Romiou
➕ 28B1

Lunch
Bunch of Grapes (££)
✉ Pissouri village
☎ 2522 1275

Pafos & the West

This is the region for those looking for some of Cyprus's quieter and more traditional areas. Pafos is a growing resort but it has not entirely lost its small town origins or its hugely important archaeological heritage. In the north are monasteries and villages. Polis, the only town of any size on the north coast, is a laid-back place. In the far northwest is the Akamas peninsula, which is the focus of environmental initiatives to protect some of the most remote and beautiful beaches in Cyprus. East of Polis is an undeveloped region with empty beaches and quiet roads up to the Green Line that marks the limit of exploration for visitors in the Greek sector of the island.

'Here [Pafos] the votaries of Aphrodite were welcomed from overseas. Here St Paul took ship after the happy outcome of his encounter with my prudent Roman predecessor. Here the crusaders and pilgrims came on their way to the Holy Land.'

SIR HUGH FOOT
last British Governor of Cyprus (1959)

———————●———————

Left: *the ruins of the Byzantine fort of Saranda Kolones, Pafos*

Pafos

The first settlement dates from the 4th century BC and Pafos played an important role in early Cypriot history. However, after the 4th century AD it declined and, though its fortunes improved marginally under British administration, it is only in the last 30 years, as transport links improved, that Pafos has seen real growth. Tourist development, in particular, took off after the construction of the international airport in 1983. However, the town remains of manageable size, with a population of 35,000, and is one of the most attractive holiday resorts on the island. The richness of its archaeology has qualified ancient Nea Pafos as a UNESCO World Heritage Site.

The modern town is split into two: upper and lower Pafos, also known as Kitma and Kato Pafos. The lower part, on the coast, contains most of the historic sites whereas the upper town contains the main commercial centre, shops and modern museums. You must bear in mind that it is quite a strenuous walk between the two parts of town, especially in the summer heat.

The lower town contains a number of archaeological sites, which are spread out across the area. Some are in

Pafos harbour, a colourful spot for sitting or strolling

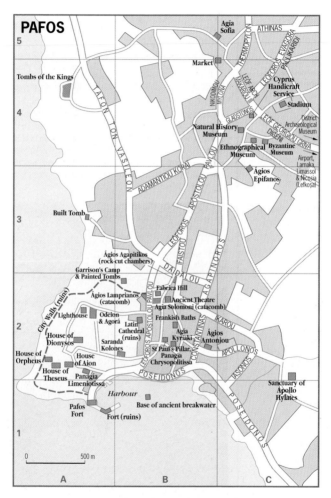

PAFOS

Agia Sofia — ATHINAS
Market
THERMOPYLON
Tombs of the Kings
LEOF ARCH MAKARIOU III
NIKODIMOU
MYLONA
GLADSTONOS
Cyprus Handicraft Service
LEOF. EVAGORA PALLIKARIDI
Stadium
District Archaeological Museum
LEOF GEORGIOU GRIVA DIGENI
Natural History Museum
Ethnographical Museum
Byzantine Museum
Airport, Larnaka, Limassol & Nicosia (Lefkoşa)
Ágios Epifanos
ADAMANTIOU KORAI
APOSTOLOU PAVLOU
Built Tomb
Ágios Agapitikos (rock-cut chambers)
LEOFOROS FAISTOU
LEOF DAIDALOU
LEOF AGAPINOROS
Garrison's Camp & Painted Tombs
Fabrica Hill
Ágios Lamprianos (catacomb)
Ancient Theatre
Agia Solomoni (catacomb)
City Walls (ruins)
Lighthouse
Odeion & Agorá
Latin Cathedral (ruins)
Frankish Baths
IKAROU
CONSTANTIAS
Ágios Antoniou
APOLLONOS
House of Dionysos
LEOFOROS APOSTOLOU PAVLOU
Saranda Kolones
Agia Kyriaki
St Paul's Pillar
JASONOS
House of Orpheus
House of Aion
House of Theseus
Panagia Chrysopolitissa
Panagia Limeniotissa
POSEIDONOS
Sanctuary of Apollo Hylates
Harbour
Base of ancient breakwater
POSEIDONOS
Pafos Fort
Fort (ruins)

0 — 500 m

A   B   C

formal areas, but do not be surprised to come across ancient ruins among modern houses.

The harbour is the focus of the lower town and is a pleasant place to stroll. It is also the haunt of Pafos's most famous resident, the pelican. Cafés string out along the seafront and there are plenty of places to eat or have a drink and watch the yachts.

What to See in Pafos

CATACOMBS

There are two underground churches in Pafos. Agía Solomoni is easily identified from the road because those who believe in the magical curative powers of the tomb attach items of clothing to the tree outside. The underground chambers include a 12th-century chapel with frescos, some of which are damaged by water and early graffiti by passing crusaders. The chambers are fairly dark and a torch can be useful, though the main chapel is lit by candles.

The second catacomb, a few minutes walk further north, is larger, but has been less well cared for and tends to be rather litter strewn.

🕇 55B2
✉ Apostolou Pavlou Avenue
🕐 Daylight hours
💲 Free

Agía Solomoni and its votive tree decked with cloths

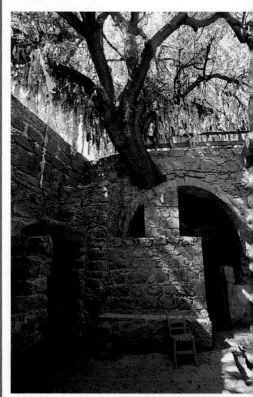

Facing page: *Pafos lighthouse towers over the restored seats of the Roman Odeion*

DISTRICT ARCHAEOLOGICAL MUSEUM

The museum houses most of the finds from local excavations. In the entrance hall is a Hellenistic sarcophagus from Pegeia and there are pottery and terracotta figures from Polis. There are also small statues and artefacts from the House of Dionysos, and sculpture and coins from the ancient city kingdoms of Cyprus. Most fascinating are articles found in room 3, including marble Roman eyeballs and clay hot-water bottles in the shape of the part of the body they were to warm.

- ✠ 55C4
- ✉ Dighenis Street
- ☎ 2694 0215
- 🕐 Mon–Fri 9–5, Sat–Sun 10–1. Closed 1 Jan, 25 Dec, Greek Orthodox Easter Sun
- 💵 Inexpensive
- 🍴 Cafés across the road (£)

ETHNOGRAPHICAL MUSEUM ⭐

This private collection of George Eliades, a local professor, ranges from neolithic to modern times. The collection includes axe heads, coins, pottery and farm implements from around the island. There is also a reconstruction of a bridal chamber displaying traditional costumes and furniture.

- ✠ 55C4
- ✉ 1 Exo Vrisis Street
- ☎ 2693 2010
- 🕐 May–Sep, Mon–Fri 9–1, 3–7, Sat 9–1, Sun 10–1; Oct–May, Mon–Fri 9–1, 2–5, Sat 9–1, Sun 10–1
- 💵 Inexpensive
- 🍴 Cafés nearby (£)

MOSAICS AT PAFOS (► 22, TOP TEN)

ODEION

This theatre has been partially restored to give an impression of how once it would have been. It was built in the 2nd century AD, during the Roman period, then suffered earthquake damage in the 7th century and was abandoned. Occasional performances are held here during the summer and details are available from the tourist office.

Just in front of the Odeion is the Agora, once the city's market place. The foundations and some of the columns survive, and there are also remains of some other municipal buildings.

- ✠ 55A2
- ✉ West of Apostolou Pavlou Avenue
- 🕐 Daylight hours
- 💵 Free
- 🍴 Cafés nearby on Apostolou Pavlou Avenue (£)

A Walk Around Pafos

Distance
3.5km

Time
1–4 hours

Start/end point
Pafos harbour
✚ 55A1
🚌 10, 15 to Coral Bay

Lunch
Cafés along the harbour (££)

Pafos lighthouse is a useful landmark when exploring the archaeological sites of the Nea Pafos headland

The walk begins at the fort at the far end of the harbour. The castle was built by the Lusignans and the dungeons and battlements are worth a visit (► 59).

Head inland on the scrubland towards the modern lighthouse until reaching the tarred road, then follow signs to the mosaics.

The mosaics are among the most impressive in the world and are amazingly well preserved (► 22). A little way back down the hill, to the left, is the Odeion (► 57), a restored Roman theatre dating from the 2nd century AD, just to the east of the lighthouse.

From the Odeion take the track east towards town, meeting the tarred road after five minutes and, soon after, the main road of Apostolou Pavlou Avenue. Turn left and 200m away on the right-hand side is the catacomb of Agía Solomoni (► 60).

The church is marked by a tree covered in handkerchiefs and is in the furthest cave.

Return down Apostolou Pavlou Avenue for about 400m, turn left into Stilis Agiou Pavlou Street to reach the site of St Paul's Pillar after about 200m.

The pillar, visible through a fence, is the site where St Paul was whipped on the order of the Romans (► 60).

Return to Apostolou Pavlou Avenue to go left. After 200m, turn right on to the road signed 'Ancient Monuments'. On the right is Saranda Kolones (Forty Columns), a ruined Byzantine fort (► 60). Cross the car park to return to the harbour.

PAFOS FORT ⭐⭐

Originally the harbour was guarded by two castles built by the Lusignans in the 13th century. Both were badly damaged when the Turks attacked in 1570, but one was subsequently restored and used by the Turks as a prison. It is open to the public and you approach across a drawbridge. The main attractions are the dungeons and battlements, from where there are excellent views across the harbour.

🔲 55A1
✉ Harbour Wall
🕐 Jun–Aug, daily 9–7:30; Sep–May, daily 9–5. Closed 1 Jan, 25 Dec, Greek Orthodox Easter Sun
💵 Cheap
🍴 Cafés on harbour front (££)

The harbour's solid fort compliments any view over the still waters

Did you know ?

The ancient city of Pafos was twice destroyed by earthquakes. It has remained susceptible to tremors and in October 1996 a tremor measuring 6.1 on the Richter scale was felt, causing landslides and some structural damage.

ST PAUL'S PILLAR AND AGÍA KYRIAKI ★

+ 55B2
✉ Stassandrou Street
⏱ Daylight hours
🆓 Free
🍴 Cafés nearby (£)

This is a small archaeological site in the back streets of Pafos, where a large number of columns and other fragments of buildings have been unearthed. Excavations are still taking place and this may mean that parts of the site will be closed off. The archaeologists are not sure what the actual buildings were in this area, although one theory is that it was a Roman Forum. Most people, however, come here to see St Paul's Pillar, which stands at the western end of the site. According to legend, St Paul was tied to this stone and given 39 lashes as a punishment for preaching Christianity. Despite this early setback, he later managed to convert the governor and the rest of the island soon followed suit.

The adjacent church of Agía Kyriaki dates from the 12th century and is still used for services.

An intricately carved, if somewhat worse for wear, floral capital in the Byzantine Museum

Did you know ?

St Barnabas brought Christianity to Cyprus. Accompanied by St Paul, he landed at Salamis then travelled to Pafos. The story of their travels is told in Acts in the Bible, which relates how St Paul blinded a local sorcerer and so impressed the Roman governor of Pafos that he converted to Christianity

SARANDA KOLONES (FORTY COLUMNS) BYZANTINE FORT ★★

+ 55B2
✉ Kyriakou Nikolaou Street
⏱ Open access
🆓 Free
🍴 Cafés nearby (££)

This castle dates from around the 7th century, although it was rebuilt in the 12th century, and was probably meant to protect the city from seaborne raiders until it was replaced by the forts on the breakwater. The remains of many of the original columns, the central keep and some of the towers on the thick outer walls can still be made out. Visitors can also see a drinking trough for horses and the ancient latrines. The site is freely open to the public who are allowed to scramble around the ruins, but those with young children should take care as some of the high walls could be dangerous.

TOMBS OF THE KINGS ⭐⭐

The 100 tombs on the site cover a wide area and are cut out of the ground with a steep drop into them, so visitors should take care when exploring. Steps lead down inside the tombs, often into a whole series of passageways. The chambers near the centre of the site do get busy and it is worth walking a little further away to those on the edge of the area, which are just as impressive. They are constructed with Doric columns, date from about the 3rd century BC and were probably used to bury the local noblemen and their families.

There are some good views over the sea and a few rocky coves are accessible after a bit of a scramble over the cliffs.

✚ 55A4
✉ 2km northwest of Pafos centre
☎ 2694 0295
🕐 Jun–Aug, daily 8:30–7:30; Sep–May, daily 8–5
💪 Inexpensive
🍴 Café on site (£)
🚌 10, 15 from Pafos

Exploring the tombs is something of an adventure

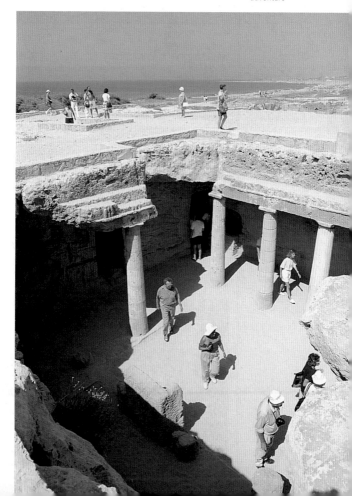

What to See in the West

ÁGIOS GEORGIOS

Ágios Georgios is a pleasant, quiet harbour with a handful of restaurants, a hotel and rooms to rent. The whole area was once a Roman settlement and some of the tombs cut out of the rock can be seen. On the headland are the remains of a 6th-century basilica.

The harbour is reached down a track from the headland and signposted Mandoulis beach. It is a very pretty place with a good stretch of sand and a view to the rocky offshore island of Geronisos.

✚ 28A2
✉ 25km north of Pafos
🍴 Restaurants overlooking the harbour (£)

ÁGIOS NEOFYTOS MONASTERY ✪✪

Saint Neofytos set up residence in caves he cut out of the hillside in 1159. The first cave he created was called the *enkleistra*, or enclosure. He then enlarged the dwelling with the addition of three new chambers, which are decorated with religious wall paintings focusing on the Crucifixion and Resurrection. Those in the sanctuary, the cave with an altar, are the best preserved. The 16th-century monastery church is dedicated to the Virgin Mary and contains a large number of paintings that depict her early life. Neofytos's bones are also kept here in a wooden sarcophagus, with his skull in a silver reliquary, which the devoted queue up to kiss.

✚ 28B2
✉ 9km north of Pafos
🕐 Apr–Sep, daily 9–1, 2–6; Oct–Mar, daily 9–4
🎫 Inexpensive
🍴 Café outside monastery
🚌 Two buses a day from Pafos lower town

AKAMAS (➤ 16, TOP TEN)

CHRYSORROGIATISSA MONASTERY ✪✪

The monastery is impressive mainly because of its setting at a height of 610m. It was founded in 1152 by a monk called Ignatius, although the main part of the monastery

✚ 28B2
✉ 3km south of Pano Panagia
🕐 Daily 9–7
🎫 Free
🍴 Café outside monastery (£)

Overhanging trees shade a flower bedecked terrace at the Chrysorrogiatissa Monastery

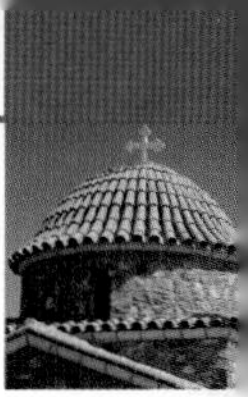

was not built until 1770. These buildings were burned down in 1821 when the Turks suspected the monks of political activity. Further trouble came in the 1950s when the abbot was murdered by EOKA terrorists who thought, erroneously, he had betrayed some of their comrades.

The monks here have shown an enterprise in reopening an old winery and now produce some excellent wines, which are on sale in the monastery. They also have icons for sale, which are painted by one of the monks. Outside the main buildings is a small café.

CORAL BAY

This is an increasingly popular resort, with shops and restaurants on the approach road and water-sports facilities on the beach. The sands are clean and pleasant and can be painfully hot to bare feet. It can also be busy.

- 28A2
- 13km north of Pafos
- 10, 15 from Pafos lower town
- Cafés on the clifftops (££)

GEROSKIPOU

The church of Agía Paraskevi, in the centre of the village, is famous throughout the island because of its distinctive five-domed plan. The building dates from the 10th-century but it has a number of decorations over the altar from the 9th century. The paintings are slightly later, from the 12th to the 15th century.

There is also a good Folk Art Museum just off the main street which contains farming and domestic implements and traditional costumes. The village is known for its 'Cyprus delight', *Loukoumi* (called 'Turkish delight' before the Turkish invasion); it is possible to watch it being made in some of the shops.

- 28B2
- 3km east of Pafos
- Agía Paraskevi: 2626 1859. Art Museum: 2694 0216
- Church: May–Oct, Mon–Sat 8–1, 2–5; Nov–Apr, Mon–Sun 8–1, 2–4. Folk Art Museum: Mon–Wed, Fri 9–2:30, Thu 9–2:30, 3–5 (closed afternoons Jul–Aug)
- Church: free. Folk Art Museum: inexpensive
- Cafés in village (£–££)
- From Pafos old town

LARA (➤ 21, TOP TEN)

PALAIA PAFOS (OLD PAFOS) KOUKLIA

The site, also known as the Sanctuary of Aphrodite, is spread over a large area. At the entrance is a restored Lusignan manor (La Cavocle) with substantial and impressive Turkish additions. It houses, in its main hall, a museum with exhibits focusing on the history of the excavation of the area and the fragments of mosaic that have been found. Its prize artefact, though, is a large black stone that stood as a manifestation of Aphrodite and was worshipped by pilgrims. The hall itself is worth a closer look as it is one of the best examples of 13th-century Gothic architecture on the island.

To the east of the museum are Roman remains, including remnants of the Sanctuary of Aphrodite, which stands around a courtyard where rituals took place. The south wing is the best preserved, and parts of the original walls still stand.

West of the sanctuary are the ruins of Roman houses, including the House of Leda; follow the path that leads to a replica of a mosaic of Leda and the Swan.

- 28B1
- 14km east of Pafos
- 2643 2180
- Jun–Aug, Mon–Fri 9–7, Sat–Sun 9–5; Sep–May, daily 9–5. Closed 1 Jan, 25 Dec, Greek Orthodox Easter Sun
- Museum: Inexpensive. Rest of the site: free

In the Know

If you only have a short time to visit Cyprus, or would like to get a real flavour of the island, here are some ideas:

Business and relaxation go together in Cyprus

10
Ways To Be A Local

Adapt to Mediterranean time – go out late, eat late, don't rush and take everything as it comes.

Wear appropriate dress when you visit churches, monasteries and mosques – no shorts or bare shoulders.

Take an afternoon siesta to escape the hot summer sun. Retreat into the shade to sleep or spin out a relaxed lunch.

Browse the bazaars and weekly fruit and vegetable markets for unrivalled value and local colour.

Buy hand-made Lefkara lace and other embroidery work. Traditionally, a Cypriot bride had to have 100 sheets and pillowcases in her dowry – but you can start a collection with just one beautiful piece.

Order a strong coffee in a traditional village coffee shop, sit back and watch the menfolk gossip and play cards and backgammon.

Linger over an alfresco dinner of *meze* dishes. With a range of up to 30 items to choose from, you can try something different every night.

Buses and service taxis are a cheap and friendly alternative to rented cars and ordinary taxis.

Locals don't get drunk in public – you shouldn't either as they will be offended if you do.

Enjoy exotic butterflies such as the Cleopatra and the two-tailed pasha.

10
Good Places To Have Lunch

Faros Restaurant
✉ Governor's Beach, east of Limassol ☎ 2563 2552. Simple food in a setting overlooking the sea. Popular with locals and visitors alike at weekends.

Mandra Tavern
✉ Dionysou Street, Kato Pafos ☎ 2623 4129. Good, traditional kebabs.

Militzis Restaurant
✉ 42 Piyale Pasa, Larnaka ☎ 2465 5867. Varied fare and first rate fish.

Napa Taverna
✉ Demokratias 15, Agía Napa ☎ 2372 1280. One of the first tavernas in Agía Napa and one of the best.

Phini Taverna
✉ Foini Village ☎ 2542 1828. Traditional dishes and fresh trout in a mountain village.

Sea Fare
✉ Seafront at Latsi ☎ 2632 2274. Wonderful seafood in a splendid harbour setting.

Tsolias
✉ Coral Bay ☎ 2662 1238. Marvellous headland situation overlooking the bay.

Petra tou Romiou Restaurant and Fish Tavern
☎ 2699 6005. Fabulous views over the celebrated rock. A short distance off the main road.

Set Fish Restaurant
✉ Kyrenia Harbour
☎ 8152336. Good
harbour position. Wide
range of fresh fish every
day. Good *kalamari*.

Vangelis
✉ Located a little outside
Paralimni on the Deryneia
road ☎ 2382 1456.
Popular with locals. For
something different try the
pigeon or rabbit

Top Activities

Sunbathing – In Cyprus all
the uncertainty is taken out
of this demanding
occupation, for the sun
shines all day every day.

Sea: Severe – There are
more ways of following a
motor boat than standing
upright on two planks of
wood. A multitude of
flexible inflatables,
including the notorious
banana, skim the waves
during high speed tows.
Some aficionados of the
foam prefer the adrenaline
boost of jet skis.

Sea: Sedate – Relaxing
pastimes include airbed
floating and the ever
popular pedalos.

Swimming – Few can
resist the warm turquoise
sea. You'll see every
swimming technique
known to man, and some
others, performed with
great virtuosity.

Luxuriating – Participants
welcome the enervating
heat and thus stimulated
take their ease at poolside,
on the terrace or the
beach. Lunch does
interfere but the conso-
lation is that a good repast
makes it that much easier
to regress into the torpid
state.

Left: *Larnaka harbour*
Top: *Troodos sunset*

Parascending – Incredibly,
people queue for this
expensive death defying
adventure. One nervous,
critical bound and it is up
into the thermals.

Golf – One has to admire
the Cypriots – nothing is
too daunting. In brown
waterless landscapes they
have created greens. Golf
in Cyprus is still in its
infancy, but who can doubt
that it will be a huge
success (➤ 112).

Hill walks – In summer it
is very hot for walking.
Nevertheless, several interesting trails have been laid
out in the Akamas and the
Troodos.

Diving – Explorations of
the wonders of the deep
are well catered for at
diving centres and some
hotels around the island.

Horse riding – There are
centres in Nicosia,
Limassol and Pafos. Riding
can be through the
countryside, including the
Troodos Mountains.

Cycling – There are scores
of bicycles for hire in all the
resorts. Main roads can be
very busy at weekends and
the tourist office advises
cyclists to avoid them at
this time.

Interesting Diversions

View the forbidden city of
Famagusta through binoc-
ulars from the roof of an
enterprising Greek
Cypriot's house in
Deryneia. There is a small
charge.

Walk the Pediaios River in
Nicosia. Join the river bed
at the ford near the
Presidential Palace and
take this unusual route into
town. Not to be undertaken
if rain is expected, as a
flash flood would be
dangerous.

Walk the Green Line in
the walled city of Nicosia.
Greek and Turkish soldiers
are almost eyeball to
eyeball and the air is tense.
Keep the camera out of
sight.

Visit the Keo distillery and
winery in Limassol. 1
Franklin Roosevelt Avenue
☎ 05 362053.

Walk a gorge in the
Akamas. Exalt Travel, Pafos
☎ 2624 3803, will arrange
a guided excursion.

Hire a pedalo or similar on
Agia Napa beach and
paddle through the unusual
weathered rock formations
at the east end of the bay.

Take a 2- or 3-day boat trip
from Limassol to the Holy
Land. Local travel agents
will provide all details (try
Louis Cruise Lines,
Limassol ☎ 2534 0000).

Visit the Grivas Museum
on the beach near Chlorakas
and see the wooden ship,
Ágios Georgios, used for
gun running during the
EOKA campaign.

See the sunrise over the
Kyrenian Hills from the
Mesaoria (central plain).
Spectacular effects reward
a spectacularly early start.

Watch the vultures on
Besparmak (Pentadaktylos)
Mountain (east of Kyrenia).
Drive to the pass, but go at
the weekend when the
nearby quarry is closed.

A Drive Around Western Cyprus

Distance
120km

Time
3½–8 hours

Start/end point
Pafos town centre
✚ 57B2

Lunch
Good restaurants in Pano
Panagía or fish restaurants in
Latsi (£–££)

Follow signs to Polis, heading out of Pafos, and after 15km turn right into the hills towards the village of Polemi.

The road runs through low hills cut into terraces to support the vines.

Some 20km after Polemi, the route reaches the village of Pano Panagia.

This is the birthplace of Archbishop Makarios (➤ 67). A further 1.5km uphill is Chrysorrogiatissa Monastery (➤ 62), which, at a height of 610m, commands some really good views of the surrounding area.

The drive then retraces the route to Pano Panagía and Asprogia, and turns right before Kannaviou on to a minor road to Fyti and Simou.

These are remote villages where traditional ways of life are still visible: do not be surprised to encounter donkeys at every turn. The villages are something of a maze, but almost all the streets lead back to the through road.

Turn northwest, rejoining the main Polis road at Loukrounou. From here it is a smooth drive down to Polis (➤ 67).

Slow but sure – who needs to hurry?

Polis has a choice of good beaches, either in the town itself, to the west in Latsi, or near the Baths of Aphrodite.

The return trip takes the western road out of Polis to the old hill village of Drouseia. The road then continues south through the hills, turning right at Kathikas, ending up at Pegeia.

This fast-growing town is famous for its springs.

Rejoin the main road at Coral Bay (➤ 63), from where it is an easy run back to Pafos.

PANO PANAGÍA ✪

The village of Pano Panagía is the place where Archbishop Makarios was born. Makarios played a key role in the campaign for independence from the British and he was the first president of Cyprus from independence in 1960 until his death in 1977.

His parent's house in the village is now a museum. It consists of two rooms, with his parent's bed, assorted crockery and family photographs. If nothing else, the house shows that Archbishop Makarios had a humble background. In the main square is a cultural centre, which displays more photographs and memorabilia from his later life as president.

✚ 28B2
✉ Pano Panagía village centre
🕐 Makarios's House: daily 10–1, 2–6. Cultural Centre: Tue–Sun 9–1, 2–5
💷 Makarios's House: donation requested. Cultural Centre: free
🍴 Many cafés in village (£)

POLIS ✪✪

The town has traditionally been the destination for backpackers and other more unconventional travellers. Most of the main restaurants and shops are found around a pedestrianised square, with a number of rooms and apartments to rent close by. There is a good beach a short walk from the town centre with a campsite adjacent.

Just east of the town, but difficult to find, is the ancient site of Marion, which was founded in the 7th century BC and developed into one of the ten city kingdoms of Cyprus.

✚ 28B2

POMOS AND TO THE EAST ✪✪

There are some wonderful quiet beaches along this section of coast, and when the road climbs up into the cliffs there are amazing views. Just beyond Pomos Point is a small fishing harbour and sheltered beach. Kokkina is a Turkish village and is inaccessible. The road detours inland and then reaches Kato Pyrgos where there is another isolated beach. No further progress is possible owing to the Turkish military.

✚ 28B2
✉ 22km northwest of Polis
🍴 Cafés at Kato Pyrgos (£)
🚌 Limited bus service from Polis to Pomos, at 11, 2, 4, 6; Sat 11, 2:30, 4

A quiet beach is worth exploring

Nicosia &
the High Troodos

Nicosia lies inland on the Mesaoria, or central plain. This location allowed the city to avoid the devastation wreaked on the coastal towns by Arab raiders. Here the plain is relatively narrow with the Kyrenian mountains to the north and the foothills of the Troodos approaching the city from the southwest.

The northern boundary is no arbitrary choice: the Green Line that divides Cyprus cuts through the heart of Nicosia. Visitors will find it a frontier they cannot cross, except at one point in Nicosia, and this privilege is reserved only for people in the south.

The other boundaries are somewhat less formidable. To the south is a splendid area of valleys and villages; Stavros in the west is a lonely forest station; Machairas Monastery and its surrounding hills make up the eastern extremity.

> *'The island has in its midst a fair city called Nicosia, which is the capital of the kingdom, well walled, with its fine gates, which are three.'*
>
> P JOAN LOPEZ
> (1770)

Left: *Selimiye Mosque, formerly the Cathedral of Santa Sophia*

Nicosia (Lefkosia/Lefkoşa)

Nicosia, the capital of Cyprus, is a divided city. The border, known as the Green Line, separates the Greek and Turkish parts of the island and runs through the middle of the city. The Greek side has all the hallmarks of a modern westernised place and is a thriving shopping and business centre, though with its ancient history still visible. The northern sector has a more dilapidated and eastern feel to it, with narrower streets and old-fashioned shops.

No man's land – the wasteland of the Green Line

Nicosia is always busy and is always hotter than the coast, so summer visitors should not plan too strenuous a programme. Fortunately the main attractions are within the old city walls and can be explored on foot. The walls themselves, built by the Venetians, still impress.

An extensive modernisation and refurbishment programme is underway in the old part of town. The pedestrianised Laïki Geitonia area is the most obvious result of that programme; it is a pleasant place to wander, with all the facilities a tourist could need, and leads into some of the older shopping streets.

There is less to see in northern Nicosia and the narrow streets make it easy to get lost. However, almost all roads eventually lead to the main sight, the Selimiye Mosque, once the Cathedral of Santa Sophia, the minarets of which dominate this part of town. There are a number of other mosques in the vicinity and a few small museums and, for the more adventurous, the Turkish Baths.

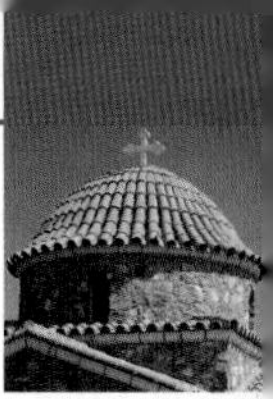

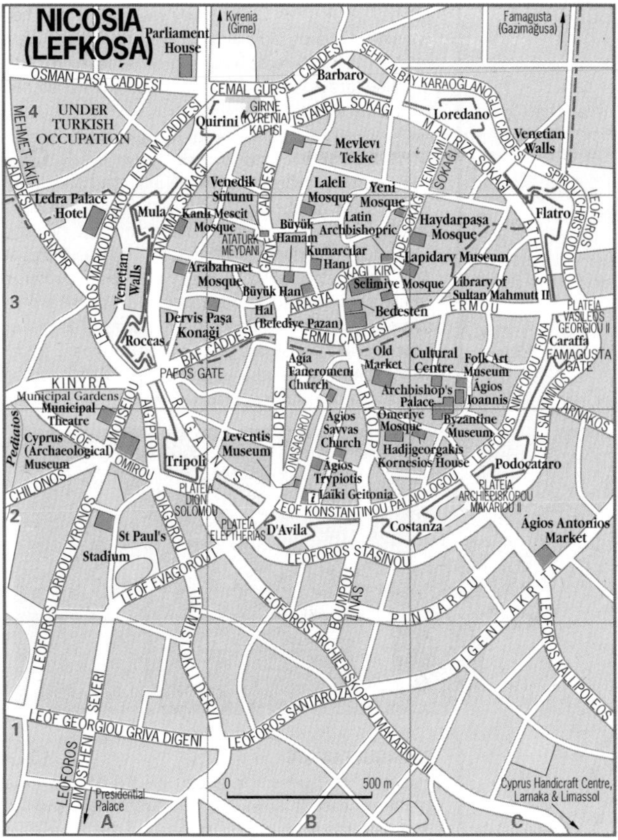
NICOSIA (LEFKOŞA)
Parliament House
Kyrenia (Girne)
Famagusta (Gazimağusa)
OSMAN PAŞA CADDESI
CEMAL GÜRSEL CADDESI
ŞEHIT ALBAY KARAOĞLANOĞLU CADDESI
UNDER TURKISH OCCUPATION
MEHMET AKIF CADDESI
Barbaro
Quirini
GIRNE (KYRENIA) KAPISI
ISTANBUL SOKAĞI
Loredano
M. ALI RIZA SOKAĞI
Venetian Walls
Mevlevi Tekke
Venedik Sütunu
Laleli Mosque
Yeni Mosque
YENICAMII SOKAĞI
Ledra Palace Hotel
Mula
Kanlı Mescit Mosque
ATATÜRK MEYDANI
Büyük Hamam
Latin Archbishopric
Haydarpaşa Mosque
Flatro
SPIROU
LEÓFOROS CHRISTODOULOU
SAIXPIR
TANZIMAT SOKAĞI
GIRNE CADDESI
Kumarcılar Hanı
KIRLIZADE SOKAĞI
Lapidary Museum
ATHINAS
Arabahmet Mosque
Büyük Han
Selimiye Mosque
Library of Sultan Mahmutt II
Venetian Walls
LEÓFOROS MARKOU DRAKOU
ARASTA
Bedesten
ERMOU
3
Derviş Paşa Konağı
Hal (Belediye Pazarı)
PLATEIA VASILEOS GEORGIOU II
Roccas
BAF CADDESI
ERMU CADDESI
Caraffa
Old Market
Cultural Centre
Folk Art Museum
FAMAGUSTA GATE
PAFOS GATE
Agia Faneromeni Church
Archbishop's Palace
Ágios Ioannis
KINYRA
Municipal Gardens
Municipal Theatre
LIDRAS
Ömeriye Mosque
Byzantine Museum
LEÓFOROS NIKIFOROU FOKA
LEOF SALAMINOS
LARNAKOS
Pediaios
Cyprus (Archaeological) Museum
LEOF MOUSEIOU
AIGYPTOU
RIGAINIS
Agios Savvas Church
Leventis Museum
TRIKOUPI
Hadjigeorgakis Kornesios House
Podocataro
Tripoli
OMIROU
ONASAGOROU
Agios Trypiotis
Laïki Geitonia
LEÓFOROS
CHILONOS
PLATEIA DION SOLOMOU
LEOF KONSTANTINOU PALAIOLOGOU
PLATEIA ARCHIEPISKOPOU MAKARIOU II
2
DIAGOROU
PLATEIA ELEFTHERIAS
D'Avila
Costanza
Ágios Antonios Market
St Paul's
Stadium
LEÓFOROS STASINOU
LEÓFOROS LORDOU VYRONOS
LEOF EVAGOROU
BOUMPOULINAS
PINDAROU
DIGENI AKRITA
LEÓFOROS ARCHIEPISKOPOU MAKARIOU III
THEMISTOKLI DERVI
LEÓFOROS KALLIPOLEOS
SEVERI
LEÓFOROS
LEOF GEORGIOU GRIVA DIGENI
LEÓFOROS SANTAROZA
1
LEÓFOROS DIMOSTHENI SEVERI
0
500 m
Presidential Palace
Cyprus Handicraft Centre, Larnaka & Limassol
A
B
C

What to See in Greek Nicosia

ÁGIOS IOANNIS CATHEDRAL ✪✪

The cathedral lies within the episcopal precinct and was built in 1662 on the site of an earlier Benedictine abbey church. It contains some fine 18th-century wall paintings and is ornately decorated throughout. It is claimed that it contained the finger of St John the Baptist until it was stolen by Mameluke raiders. The cathedral, now used for all official religious occasions, is smaller than one might expect of a building of such importance and is best visited early before the crowds arrive.

- 71C3
- Archbishopric
- Mon–Fri 8–12, 2–4, Sat 8–12
- Free
- Cafés nearby (£)

71C2
Archbishopric
2243 0008
Mon–Fri 9–4:30, Sat 9–1
Moderate
Cafés nearby (£)

Antiquities in the Cyprus Museum

71A2
Museum Street
2286 5864
Mon–Sat 9–5, Sun 10–1.
Closed 1 Jan, 25 Dec,
Greek Orthodox Easter
Sun
Moderate
Café opposite (££)

ARCHBISHOP MAKARIOS CULTURAL CENTRE (BYZANTINE MUSEUM)

The most important exhibits in the museum are the 6th-century Kanakaria Mosaics, which were thought lost when they were stolen from their church on the Karpas peninsula in northern Cyprus. They were recovered when offered for sale on the international art market and were returned to this purpose-built wing of the museum. Also on show are a large number of icons from churches around the island.

CYPRUS MUSEUM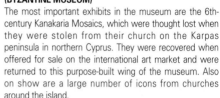

The museum houses most of the important finds from sites across Cyprus – neolithic artefacts, Bronze Age vases and clay figurines, Mycenaean objects from Kourion and sophisticated pottery. Two thousand figurines found at Agía Iríni are displayed as they were found, gathered around a single altar. A wide range of sculptures are on show, as well as a huge bronze statue of Emperor Septimius and the famous green-horned god from Enkomi. There are impressive artefacts from Salamis, some mosaics and a reconstruction of a rock cut tomb.

71C3
Leoforus Athinon
2243 0877
Mon–Fri 10–1, 4–7, (5–8
Jun–Aug)
Free
Cafés nearby (£)

71C2
Patriarchou Grigoriou
Street
2243 2578
Mon–Fri 9–5, Sat 10–1
Inexpensive
Cafés nearby (£)

FAMAGUSTA GATE

This was the main entrance into the old city from the south and east. It is set into the historic walls and has been restored to house a cultural centre that is used for exhibitions and other events. The whole area is now attracting artists who have set up studios in many of the old buildings.

HADJIGEORGAKIS KORNESIOS HOUSE (ETHNOGRAPHICAL MUSEUM)

This house belonged to the great dragoman of Cyprus, Hadjigeorgakis, at the end of the 18th century. The dragoman was a translator, an important and powerful role at that period. The museum contains a number of artefacts from the dragoman's life, displayed in reconstructions of some of the original rooms, along with letters and documents prepared by Hadjigeorgakis.

A Walk Around Nicosia

Start at Laïki Geitonia (➤ 74), the pedestrianised shopping area, and find Ippocratous Street immediately to the north.

Walk west and pass the Leventis Museum (➤ 74) to turn right into Onasagorou Street. In 250m there is an awkward junction, but generally proceed straight on down Mouson Street, after a slight move to the right. Continue for about 100m before turning right at the junction where there is a school on the corner. This is Lefkonos Street, and it crosses Aischylou Street, leading into Trikoupi Street. Turn right for 200m to reach Tylliria Square.

The Ömerye Mosque lies directly ahead (➤ 74), and a short distance to the east down Patriarchos Gregorios Street is the Hadjigeorjakis Kornesios House (➤ 72).

From the house it is 50m to the left turn into Zinonos Kitieos Street.

At the far end of this road is the Archbishop's Palace, a large, neo-Venetian style building with a huge statue of Archbishop Makarios outside. The Byzantine Museum (➤ 72) and Ágios Ioannis Cathedral (➤ 71) are just beyond the palace on the left.

Continue northward into a pedestrianised area, down Agiou Ioannou Street to turn right and soon left along Antigonou Street. There is a mosque ahead. Turn right on to Ammochostou Street.

At the far end is Famagusta Gate (➤ 72) and it is then possible to follow the road around the Venetian Walls (➤ 86). There are some pleasant, well-watered gardens within the former moat outside the walls.

The main road leads back to Laïki Geitonia, passing the Costanza Bastion where the Bayraktar Mosque can be seen.

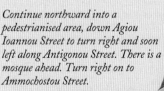

Distance
3km

Time
2–4 hours

Start/end point
Laïki Geitonia
🔲 71B2
🚌 152 from Limassol/Pafos, 146 from Larnaka stop at Plateia Dionysios Solomou bus station just outside the walls

Lunch
Many restaurants in the Laïki Geitonia area (£)

The statue of Makarios outside the Archbishop's Palace

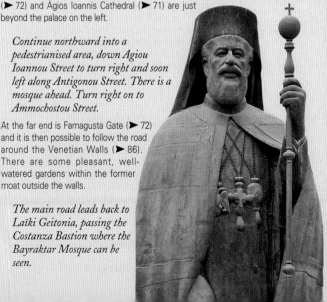

71B2
Within old city walls, northeast of Plateía Eleftheria Square
Many cafés (££)

LAÏKI GEITONIA

This is a pedestrianised area of old Nicosia where traditional old buildings have been restored, shops refurbished and trees planted. It is specifically aimed at the tourist, with a whole range of restaurants, craft shops and the tourist office, as well as a small jewellery museum.

The old shopping streets of Ledra and Onasagoras that lead out of the Laïki Geitonia area are also interesting places to wander. Rather more traditional shops are found on these streets and at their northern end are the sandbags that mark the Green Line.

71B2
Ippokratous Street
2266 1475
Tue–Sun 10–4:30. Closed 1 Jan, 25 Dec, Greek Orthodox Easter Sun
Free
Café in basement (££)

LEVENTIS MUSEUM

This museum, in Laïkï Geitonia, is well set out and modest in size. Medieval finds are in the basement, some of which were uncovered when the building was being restored. The first floor deals with the period 2300 BC to the Turkish period and the ground floor covers the British colonial time as well as the city's recent history. The documentation from this later period is particularly interesting although the commentaries can be a little partisan.

71B2
Trikoupi Street
Any reasonable hour and when there is prayer
Free
Cafés nearby (£)

ÖMERIYE MOSQUE

As with many of the city's mosques this building was originally a church, converted in 1571 by Mustafa Paşa, the occupying Turkish general. He believed that the visit of the Muslim prophet Omar should be commemorated, and as a result the minaret was added and the old Lusignan tombstones used to cover the floor. The mosque is still used as a place of worship, but the public can climb the minaret from where there are splendid views across the city.

> ### *Did you know ?*
>
> *The Ledra Palace Hotel used to be the main luxury hotel in Nicosia. Now standing on the Green Line, it is home to British United Nations troops and is marked with bullet holes from the 1974 conflict. It is used for meetings between the two sides, both official and unofficial.*

WALLED CITY (▶ 23, TOP TEN)

What to See in Turkish Nicosia

BÜYÜK HAMAM

This was once the Church of St George, built in the 14th century and subsequently converted to a bathhouse by the Turks. The main room is domed, the floor well below street level. On Fridays it is women only, other days men only. Should it be locked the café owner on the west side has the key.

➕ 71B3
✉ Mousa Orfenbey Sokagi
🕐 Jun–Sep, daily 7:30–1, 4–6; Oct–May, daily 8–1, 2–6
✋ Free entry. Baths: moderate
🍴 Café next door (£)

BÜYÜK HAN ★★

The building was commissioned in 1572 by Mustafa Paşa, the first Ottoman governor of Cyprus. It was a simple inn, complete with stables and a wonderful little mosque in the courtyard. Perhaps the nadir of its fortunes was when it became Nicosia's central prison in 1893.

Its days of neglect are now over – the Department of Antiquities has restored it, albeit as a museum.

➕ 71B3
✉ Arasta Sokagi
🕐 Mon–Fri 9–4
✋ Inexpensive

LAPIDARY MUSEUM ★

The building is on two levels, perhaps once the home of a wealthy Venetian family. Assorted wooden relics from mosques and churches display fine carving.

In the courtyard is a random selection of Corinthian capitals, carved stone heads and a section of a beautiful rose window.

➕ 71C3
✉ Northeast of the Selimiye Mosque
🕐 Jun–Sep, daily 7.30–2, 4–6; Oct–May 8–1, 2–5. If locked, try custodian at the Library of Sultan Mahmut II across the road
✋ Inexpensive

Büyük Han's little mosque, now being restored to its former splendour

71B4
Girne Caddesi
Jun–Sep, Mon–Fri
7:30–2; Oct–May 9–1,
2–4:45
Inexpensive

MEVLEVI TEKKE
(ETHNOGRAPHICAL MUSEUM)

This was the home of the whirling dervishes, a sect founded in the 13th century. The rooms have a simple elegance, complete with a splendid minstrels' gallery looking down on where the dervishes, heads lowered in contemplation, would stretch out their arms and spin at ever increasing speed. In 1925 Kemal Ataturk forbade such dancing in an attempt to modernise Turkish culture. After 20 years the ruling was relaxed and the dance celebrated once more. To one side is a collection of costumes, wedding dresses and musical instruments. Adjoining is a long mausoleum of 15 tombs, resting places of important dervishes.

Above: *an engraved stone at Mevlevi Tekke*
Right: *sixteen dervishes perform the dance*

71B3
Selimiye Sokagi
Daily
Free

SELIMIYE MOSQUE

This impressive building was a Christian masterpiece before conversion to a mosque of the Ottoman Turks, the most important in Cyprus. The elevations of magnificent windows, portals and buttresses are worryingly discordant, the reason – the soaring minarets. They are landmarks in the walled city, and their imposition on the west front by the Turks reflects the momentous events of 1570–1 when they subjugated the city.

The original cathedral was started in 1209 and substantially completed 117 years later. In reality it was never quite finished, work carrying on long after the consecration.

Everything changed with the arrival of the Turks. All the overt Christian decoration of the cathedral was destroyed. Soon work was started on the minarets and the building became the Cathedral of Santa Sophia until the name was changed to the Selimiye Mosque in 1954.

What to See in the High Troodos

ÁGIOS IRAKLEIDIOS ✪
The monastery was founded in the Byzantine era, and it is dedicated to the saint who guided St Paul and St Barnabas to nearby Tamassos during their missionary travels. St Irakleidios lived in a cave, and the first church was built around it. His skull is kept in the present building in a silver reliquary, and many believe it has miraculous powers to heal the sick.

The complex is now a convent. It dates from 1773 and is a simple construction of good appearance, enhanced by excellent gardens. These are meticulously tended by the nuns and in summer are an oasis of greenery and colour in the barren landscape.

➕ 28C2
✉ Near the village of Politikon
◷ Rarely open to casual visitors
💷 Free
🍴 Café opposite (£)

ASINOU CHURCH (PANAGÍA FORVIOTISSA) ✪✪
The fame of this church is such that it is quite a surprise to find it so tiny, hidden on a north-facing hillside of eucalyptus and pine trees. A steep clay-tiled outer roof protects the vulnerable Byzantine dome and treasures within.

Asinou remains unscathed after 900 years. The frescos are the best of Cyprus's painted churches, the earliest dating back to the 12th century. They were added to over the years and culminate in the powerful work by refugee painters from Asia Minor.

Christ is depicted in the sanctuary and the dome of the narthex, gazing down. All around, the rank and file are beautifully illustrated.

➕ 28C2
✉ Near Nikitari
◷ Ask in Nikitari for the priest with the key
💷 Free

Ornate interior of Ágios Irakleidios

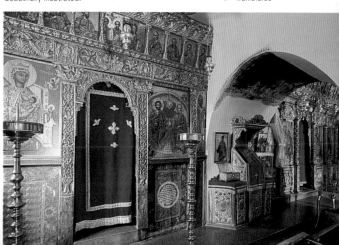

Faith is alive and well in Cyprus: a new church at Kakopetria

Did you know ?

In the 15th century the Venetians built a series of bridges over the rivers that cut into the Troodos Mountains. They were for pack animals, particularly camels, to carry copper ore from Mylikouri, Kaminaria, and Foini, high in the hills, to Pafos for export.
Alas the camel has gone the way of the export trade. The last census in 1965 counted only 90. Today there is perhaps one, or possibly two, giving rides to holidaymakers in Pafos.

✚ 28C2

Ágios Nikolaos tis Stegis
✉ Tue–Sat 9–4, Sun 11–4
🎫 Free
🍴 Several cafés (£–££)

KAKOPETRIA ✪
The village stands high in the poplar lined Solea Valley. As hill villages go, it is quite large and a favourite holiday resort of Cypriots. They come in the summer to see relatives or to escape the suffocating lowland heat. It is certainly not a smart place, the buildings are generally old or ramshackle or both, but it has charm and some traditional dwellings are being restored.

Three kilometres up the valley is the celebrated church of Ágios Nikolaos tis Stegis with its famous roof. Below the town, at Galata, are the tiny churches of Panagía Eleousa and Panagía Theotokos, looking like country barns, with their roofs nearly to the ground.

KYKKOS MONASTERY (➤ 20, TOP TEN)

A Drive into The Troodos Mountains

For Pafos visitors, the drive proper starts 17km towards Limassol.

Take the left turn at the Xeros River for Nikokleia, Mamonia and Ágios Georgios. It is a slow and splendid 55km up to Platres (Pano), through orchards and farmland.

The route from Limassol begins about 13km to the west, immediately after Erimi.

Take the road right to Kantou, Souni and Agios Amvrosios. About 37km of pleasant uphill driving leads to Omodos village, now a popular tourist attraction. It is another 14km to meet up with the Pafos travellers at Platres.

Traverse the confusing streets of Platres to reach the Nicosia–Limassol highway and go left up to Troodos village – about 7km. The route runs for 11km along the minor road to Prodromos, the highest village in Cyprus. Take a short detour to Mount Olympus (► 80) if time permits.

Soon after Prodromos the descent becomes dramatic, as the road twists and turns above the abyss.

This is a cherry-growing area, and its main villages – Pedoulas, Moutoullas and Kalopanagiotis – are reached in succession. Moutoullas is also famous for its spring water. After the excitement of the hairpin bends, it is a simple run of about 8km before sweeping east towards Linou and the Limassol–Nicosia highway.

Turn right for Troodos/Limassol and climb the mountain. Kakopetria (► 78), after 14km, is worth the short detour. At Troodos village, Limassol-bound travellers simply continue for about 55km, via Trimiklini and Pano Polemedia. Pafos-bound drivers can turn off at Platres to reverse their route via Mandria, Ágios Nikolaos and Mamonia.

Distance
Limassol – 200km
Pafos – 220km

Time
5–8 hours

Start/end point
Limassol or Pafos
✚ 28B1

Lunch
Caruralli
✉ Pedoulas
☎ 2295 2441

Omodos's main street may have lost some of its character but not its sleepy afternoons

MACHAIRAS MONASTERY ✪✪

☩ 28C2
✉ Near Fikardou, eastern Troodos
🕐 Rarely open to casual visitors
🖐 Free
🍴 Cafés nearby (£)

The monastery was founded in the 12th century and grew around an icon of the Virgin Mary. Successive fires destroyed the original church and its wall paintings and in 1892 the entire monastery was burned to the ground.

The present building dates from the early 20th century, and its elevations are fortress-like, broken up with wooden balconies. Within is an impressive iconostasis, illuminated by chandeliers. On feast days rituals take place starting early and culminating at midnight with the abbot emerging with the holy fire, a glowing candle.

The simple interior of Machairas Monastery is in contrast to the unusual external elevations

Outside a track leads down the wooded valley to the cave of Grigoris Afxentiou, second in command of EOKA during the uprising against the British. In 1957 a shepherd betrayed him and British soldiers surrounded the cave entrance. Afxentiou chose to fight, dying eight hours later in his hideout.

MOUNT OLYMPUS ✪

☩ 28B2
✉ 55km from Limassol, 97km from Nicosia
🍴 Cafés in Troodos village 4km away (£)

At 1,951m above sea level, the summit of Mount Olympus is the highest ground in Cyprus. It is not an inaccessible peak, as a narrow road winds towards the top, stopping just below the summit at an unappealing radar dome and other military facilities. As a mountain it is thereby compromised. Nevertheless it is worth the journey simply to gaze out over Cyprus, the land dramatically falling away.

This magnificent view is even better in winter. It is an unforgettable experience to stand in deep snow, bathed in sunlight, and look over to Morfou Bay and on to the Taurus Mountains of Turkey.

Dawn over the Troodos Mountains, splendid but deceptively cold – temperatures on the high ground are close to freezing

Did you know ?

The adverse fortune of recent years of one of Cyprus's oldest, shyest and most distinctive residents is now over. The moufflon, the largest wild animal in Cyprus, was declared a protected species in 1995. This deliverance was timely – the numbers of the impressive horned sheep had been reduced to just 300 by relentless hunting.

PANAGÍA TOU ARAKA

The paintings in this church are marvellous. Unfortunately the drive to get there is long and tiring, albeit through superb scenery. To confound matters, the church is generally locked, admission being by courtesy of the priest normally found in the village of Lagoudera.

The church retains the most complete series of wall paintings of the Byzantine period on the island and they were recently restored, courtesy of UNESCO. They represent the metropolitan classicizing school in full bloom. Even visitors who know little of this Byzantine style will surely appreciate their magnificence.

✚ 28C2
✉ Lagoudera
🕐 Sun, courtesy of the priest in Lagoudera
🎫 Free
🍴 Café in nearby village (£)

The North

This is the Turkish-controlled part of Cyprus, underpopulated compared to the remainder of the island. Change is slow in coming, perhaps due to the easy-going temperament of the Turkish Cypriot, but certainly attributable in part to the embargoes imposed by most of the world.

Whatever the objectives of these impositions they cannot detract from the magnificent scenery, and they have certainly so far prevented destructive mass tourism.

Along the north shore the spectacular Kyrenian Hills run unbroken for 90km. To the south the land is flat, opening out into the Mesaoria east of Nicosia. In summer it is impressively barren: in spring the colour has to be seen to be believed.

The fabled Karpasia is spectacular, with the blue Mediterranean visible to north and south of the narrow peninsula.

' Cyprus is the farthest of the Christian lands. All ships and all wares … must needs come first to Famagusta and pilgrims from every land journeying to countries over sea must touch at Cyprus. '

CLAUDE DELAVAL COBHAM
Excerpta Cypria (1908)

Famagusta (Gazimağusa)

The city is divided, although not between Greek and Turk. Varosha, the new town, with its painted hotels bordering the sandy beach, is closed to all but the military. It has been so since 1974. Visitors must therefore concentrate on the walled city. They are adequately compensated in that it is one of the finest surviving examples of medieval military architecture in existence.

The fruit stall's simple awning gives protection against the searing midday heat

To pass through the massive walls is to pass through history, from the time of the Lusignans, Genoese and Venetians to the bloody siege by the Turks in 1570–1. They stormed the walls and all Cyprus was theirs for over 300 years. The scene was set for the troubles of today.

In the narrow streets shops are unchanged by time or fashion. Dark interiors hide a miscellany of goods. The town can be a bustling place, of noise and activity, but more often it is calm, the residents going about their business in a relaxed manner. They may not be as outgoing as their Greek Cypriot countrymen in the south, but they are equally courteous and helpful.

There is much unexpected open space in all directions: a chaotic panorama of unkempt gardens and scrubland where palm trees shade ancient domed churches. Crumbling examples of splendid medieval buildings are all around. The battered minaret and massive buttress of Lala Mustafa Paşa mosque form an impressive landmark for those who get lost in these exotic surroundings.

FAMAGUSTA (GAZIMAĞUSA)

0   200   400 m

Del Mozzo · Diamante
Signoria
Carmelite Church (St Mary's) · Biddulph's Gate · St George of the Latins · Citadel (Othello's Tower)
Martinengo
Salamis · San Luca · Tanner's Mosque · Twin Churches · Sea Gate · Harbour
Pulacazara · Nestorian Church · Market · Lala Mustafa Paşa Mosque (St Nicholas Cathedral)
Palazzo de Proveditore
Moratto · Djafer Paşa Baths & Fountain · St Peter & St Paul · St George of the Greeks · Agios Nicolas
Nicosia (Lefkosa) · Diocare · Agia Zoni · Canbulat Bastion & Museum
Rivettina or Ravelin · Venetian Walls · Land Gate · Santa Napa · Andruzzi · Camposanto
Monument of Victory

What to See in Famagusta

LALA MUSTAFA PAŞA MOSQUE ✪✪✪

84B2
Naim Efendi Sokagi
Daily
Free
Café opposite west front (£)

The building has been a mosque for over 400 years, but, the architecture is of a Gothic cathedral. There is a single minaret, well executed but certainly out of place. Even so, you can still admire the splendid six-light window of the west front. Three portals lead to the impressive interior, where Moslem simplicity has allowed the fine nave to survive the loss of its Christian decoration.

Lala Mustafa was the victorious commander of the Ottoman Turks when they broke into Famagusta in 1571. Surprisingly, the mosque only received his name in 1954, before which it was called the Mosque of Santa Sophia.

ST GEORGE OF THE GREEKS ✪

84C2
Mustafa Ersu Sokagi
Daily
Free

This is a substantial church, if deteriorating significantly. It was built in 1359, probably in opposition to the Cathedral of St Nicholas (now Lala Mustafa Paşa Mosque). The three apses are traditionally semicircular. A dome covered the middle section of the church, but by all accounts it collapsed under cannon fire in 1571. Some wall paintings survive, the best being in the eastern apse.

A Famagusta Walk

The walk starts at the Land Gate entrance of the historic walled city.

Istiklal Caddesi is directly opposite and should be followed, taking care not to lose it at the three-way junction after 130m.

About 130m further, on the left, is the Church of St Peter and St Paul (➤ 86), once a public library.

A right turn along Sinan Paşa Sokagi leads to the Palazzo de Proveditore (Venetian Palace).

From here it is a small distance to Namik Kemal Zindani (Square), overlooked by the magnificent west front of Lala Mustafa Paşa Mosque (➤ 84).

A short retreat (to the west) picks up Kisla Sokagi, and in 130m are the twin churches (now restored) of the Knights Templar and Knights Hospitaller. Immediately beyond the churches the road turns right, to the northeast, and in 120m Cafer Paşa Sokagi.

At the eastern end stand the ruined, but impressive buttresses and lancet windows of St George of the Latins. The Citadel (Othello's Tower) is a short distance to the north and should not be bypassed.

The walk continues alongside the sea wall, down Canbulat Yolu, to reach the splendid Sea Gate after 200m.

In another 160m, a short detour along Mustafa Ersu Sokagi brings you to the substantial Church of St George of the Greeks (➤ 84). Returning to the main road, the Canbulat Museum is reached in 300m.

The return to the Land Gate is about 1,100m. Pass outside the walls at the Canbulat Museum and follow the south wall.

Distance
2.75km

Time
1–3½ hours

Start/end point
Land Gate
➕ 84B1

Lunch
Café opposite west front of Lala Mustafa Paşa Mosque (£)

The Land Gate and Ravelin, scene of desperate fighting in the great siege of 1570–1

84B2
Abdullah Paşa Sokagi
Mon–Fri 7:30–2;
Oct–May 8–1, 2–5. May
be closed for restoration
Free
Cafés nearby (£)

84B1
Citadel: Jun–Sep, daily
10–5; Oct–May, daily
9–1, 2–4.45. Museum:
Jun–Sep, daily 9–5;
Oct–May, daily 9–1,
2–4.45. Elsewhere no
restrictions
Citadel and museum:
inexpensive. Elsewhere
free
Cafés nearby (£)

*A Venetian winged lion
guards the entrance to
the Citadel, or Othello's
Tower*

ST PETER AND ST PAUL (SINAN PAŞA MOSQUE)

The Gothic church is distinctive for its spectacular flying buttresses. It was subsequently used as a mosque, as the ruined minaret in one corner testifies, and has also served as the municipal library. At other times it stored potatoes and grain and was known as the wheat mosque. On entering, the reason for the massive buttresses is apparent – the nave is of tremendous height, exerting a colossal force on the outside walls.

VENETIAN WALLS

The original plan of the town was laid out by the Lusignans, but, when the Venetians took over in 1489 they completely renovated the enclosing walls. Experts in military architecture, they lowered the walls but increased the thickness, taking out all features that were vulnerable to cannon fire.

Any tour of the fortifications should take into account the great heat of summer and the low parapets everywhere.

The Citadel should be visited. It is also known as Othello's Tower, a name derived from Shakespeare's play, set in a 'seaport in Cyprus.' Four great cylindrical towers guard the corners of the Citadel. The carving over the entrance is an impressive winged lion of St Mark. The great hall is a massive vaulted chamber.

Taking a clockwise circuit of the walls, the Sea Gate, 200m southeast, is the next place of interest. The gate's portcullis is part of the original Venetian work.

In another 500m is the Canbulat Gate and bastion (Canbulat was a Turkish hero of the siege), now a museum. Muskets and swords are displayed next to period dresses finished with fine embroidery.

Three bastions on the south wall lead to the Land Gate, the main entrance to the town. It is part of the Ravelin, a bastion considered impregnable when built, but later found wanting as its ditch offered cover to the enemy.

What to See in The North

BELLAPAIS ABBEY ✪✪✪

The location of the abbey on the northern slopes of the Kyrenia Hills is marvellous. Far below are almond and olive groves on the fertile coastal plain with Kyrenia in miniature to the west.

Augustinian canons founded the abbey at the end of the 12th century, its importance lasting for some 300 years. Substantial parts collapsed long ago. The cloister is half ruined, flamboyant tracery hangs down from the pointed arches.

On the north side is the refectory, where the vault appears to spring lightly from the supporting capitals. Six tall windows look out on to the northern shore, and an exquisite pulpit, reached by an intricate stair ingeniously constructed in the thickness of the wall.

The 13th-century church is generally locked, but the custodian may open it on request.

In 1995 forest fires swept through the Kyrenian Hills, advancing rapidly on Beylerbeyi, the village where the author Lawrence Durrell lived from 1953 to 1956. In his celebrated *Bitter Lemons* he had written 'two things spread quickly; gossip and a forest fire'. It was only good fortune and the skill of the firefighters that prevented the destruction of Beylerbeyi in July 1995.

🜊 28C3
✉ Bellapais (Beylerbeyi) village
🕐 Jun–Sep 9–7; Oct–May 9–1, 2–4:45
🍽 Inexpensive
🍴 Café at the gate (£)

The church, the oldest and best preserved part of the abbey, is occasionally used for services

---

Did you know ?

Lawrence Durrell passed some of his leisure time drinking coffee and telling stories under the Tree of Idleness in Beylerbeyi (Bellapais). He warned against this relaxation if work remained to be done. Two adjoining cafés now lay claim to the tree, to the amusement of the late Sabri Tahir, who helped Durrell to buy his village house. He thought they were arguing over the wrong tree.

29E3
Near Kantara village
Jun–Sep, daily 10–5;
Oct–May, daily 9–1
Inexpensive
Cafés in Kantara village
(£)

KANTARA

Kantara is the most easterly of the great Lusignan fortresses of the northern shore. At 600m above sea level, its walls crown rocky crags, with the north shore way below and stretching into the distance.

The location at the eastern end of the Kyrenia Hills gave the garrison control of the Karpasia peninsula. Visitors can, in a brief panorama, survey this unique landscape in its entirety.

Café terraces on Kyrenia's lovely waterfront

Most of the castle is a ruin, although the formidable outer wall is substantially intact. Entrance is gained through a ruined barbican and two towers. Steps lead on to vaulted chambers and medieval latrines. On the highest ground, only a Gothic window remains.

28C3
Cafés around the harbour
(£–££)

KYRENIA (GIRNE)

Kyrenia is unmatched in the rest of Cyprus. This eulogy attributes nothing to Kyrenia town and environs. It is all to do with the harbour and its magnificent setting. Certainly the old buildings of the quayside, with the exception of the customs houses, have all been reconstituted as restaurants and bars, nethertheless everything seems just perfect, day or night.

A huge cylindrical bastion from Venetian times forms the east end of the harbour, a minaret rises up in the middle ground and an Anglican spire in the west. Mountain ridges and summits run unbroken into the hazy distance.

A Drive from Kyrenia to Kantara

The outward leg of this drive has few route problems, staying close to the magnificent shore most of the way.

Drivers should take the coast road east out of Kyrenia, towards Ágios Epiktitos (Çatalköy).

In colonial days the British set up mile posts and all beaches of significance on this north shore were described by the distance to Kyrenia. Six Mile Beach (also Acapulco), Eight Mile Beach and Twelve Mile Beach are all on the route. The latter is the longest sandy stretch on the coast, but it cannot be seen from the road.The villages of Karaagac, Esentepe, Bahceli and Tatlisu are all 2 or 3km off the main route. A detour to Tatlisu is recommended.

From the Tatlisu junction it is another 19km to reach the south turn to Kaplica. Now the road climbs steeply up to the village of Kantara.

Its castle (➤ 88), another 6km along the mountain ridge, is certainly worth visiting.

Return to the village, then start the rapid descent to Turnalar, Yarkoy and on to the pleasant village of Boğaz, overlooking Famagusta Bay. The return section of the drive is southwest for 4km, before turning west to İskele, the birthplace of Grivas, the EOKA leader.

The large village of Geçitkale, in a parched landscape in summer, is another 19km on a broad highway.

A narrow road runs west, and after about 16km follow Lefkoşa (Nicosia) signs to reach the main highway. After 12km, turn right for Kyrenia (Girne) to ascend rapidly to the pass at 750m above sea level, with Beşparmak Mountain looming large to the right.

Now it is all downhill towards the sea, with another 12km along the coast to Kyrenia.

Take a well-earned rest at a harbourside café.

Distance
190km

Time
4½–7½ hours

Start/end point
Kyrenia
28C3

Lunch
Cafés in Kantara village (£)

Kyrenia Castle
- ✉ Harbour
- 🕐 Jun–Sep, daily 9–7; Oct–May, 9–1, 2–4:45
- ✋ Inexpensive

The origins of the **castle** are Lusignan, but it was the Venetians who made it impregnable. Inside, sunlight streams down from hidden windows and openings. Entry into the complex structure is over the moat, now dry, to reach a gatehouse. Progress is then up a ramp, passing a small Byzantine chapel and then on to the northwest tower. Here is the tomb of Sadik Paşa, killed in 1570 during the Turkish conquest of Cyprus. Various routes can be taken to complete a tour of the castle, care being needed to keep clear of the unguarded drops.

The shipwreck museum within the castle should not be missed. It houses one of the oldest surviving ships, raised from the seabed in 1968–9. The blackened hull, astonishingly well preserved, is more than 2,300 years old.

ST HILARION CASTLE (► 24, TOP TEN)

SALAMIS (► 25, TOP TEN)

SOLI   ✪✪

A detail of a mosaic floor at Soli

- 🟥 28B2
- ✉ Near Gemikonagi
- 🕐 Jun–Sep, daily 9–7; Oct–May, daily 9–1, 2–4:45
- ✋ Inexpensive

The founders of Soli came from Greece and they created a city destined to play a major role in the struggle against Persian rule in the 5th and 4th centuries BC. However, only the later work of the Romans survives. They cut a theatre out of a rocky hillside overlooking Morfou Bay; today, most of this substantial work is a reconstruction. Near the road are the remains of a colonnade leading to an agora. Some mosaics survive, the bird representations being most impressive.

The wealth of Soli lay with its copper, mined from the surrounding hills. Boats from the city's harbour, long silted up, carried the metal to various parts of the Mediterranean.

VOUNI   ✪✪

- 🟥 28B3
- ✉ Near Gemikonagi
- 🕐 Jun–Sep, daily 10–5; Oct–May, daily 9–1, 2–4:45
- ✋ Inexpensive

The road to ruined Vouni Palace spirals spectacularly upwards, a splendid area where the Troodos Mountains meet the northern shore. A series of terraces, swept bare by time, climb the hillside. The palace was clearly a substantial construction, with apartments, baths and courtyards. Little is known but it was built in the 5th century BC by a pro-Persian king from Marion, possibly to counter the power of nearby Soli, a city loyal to the Greeks. The baths have a water system comparable to those of the Romans, but it is centuries earlier. At the top of the hill are the ruins of the Greek-style Temple of Athena.

Where To...

Above: *Ágios Irakleidios fresco*
Right: *Greek Orthodox monk at Agía Ekaterina*

91

Larnaka &
the Southeast

Prices

Prices are approximate, based on a three-course meal for one, without drinks and service:

Republic of Cyprus

£	= up to C£7
££	= C£7–C£14
£££	= over C£14

Northern Cyprus

£	= up to TL1,800,000
££	= TL1,800,000–TL3,600,000
£££	= over TL3,600,000

Agía Napa

Le Bistro d' Hier (££)
The menu changes daily but retains a mainly French selection. Vegetarian food is available on request.
✉ 11 Odyseos Elitis Street,
☎ 2372 1838 🕐 Daily until late

Georgis Flambé (£)
Tourist menu in alfresco surroundings.
✉ 9 Ippocratou Street
☎ 2372 1504 🕐 Daily until late. Closed in winter

Oleander Taverna (££)
One of the oldest establishments in the resort. It has a reputation for good food and service.
✉ 10 Kryou Street ☎ 2372 1951 🕐 Daily

Royal Viking (££)
The steaks are certainly good, but so are the local dishes and reasonably priced specialities.
✉ 31 Nisi Avenue
☎ 2372 2378 🕐 Daily

Villa Fioria (£££)
Italian menu prepared to a high standard.
✉ Kryou Street ☎ 2372 3923
🕐 Daily

Larnaka

Kantara (££)
Well prepared and presented international cuisine to suit all tastes.
✉ Selinis 1, Dhekalia Road (opposite Karpasiana Hotel)
☎ 2464 5783 🕐 Daily

Megalos Pefkos (££)
Good location on the shore by the fort. Fresh fish, Cyprus *meze* and steaks, plus a free drink. Vegetarian choice.
✉ Ankara Street ☎ 2462 8566 🕐 Daily until late

Monte Carlo (££)
Overlooking the bay with a nice line in traditional Cypriot dishes, *meze* a speciality. Stylishly decorated place with a balcony.
✉ 28 Piale Pashia Street
☎ 2465 3815 🕐 Daily

1900 Art Café (£)
Very good local cuisine in an attractively restored old house.
✉ Stassinou 6 ☎ 2465 3027
🕐 Daily 9–2, 6–12

Rendez Vous Creperie (££)
Worth trying the fondue here as it is just as good as the pancakes.
✉ Dhekalia Road, Oroklini
☎ 2464 4532 🕐 Daily for dinner. Closed Tue, Oct–May

Retro (££)
Good Cypriot fare, as well as pizzas, spaghetti, beers and cakes.
✉ Francis Court, 7 Gr. Afxentiou Avenue ☎ 2465 6268
🕐 Daily

Tudor Inn (££)
Steaks served in a variety of ways with excellent sauces. Vegetarian dishes are also available.
✉ 28a Lala Mustafa ☎ 2462 5608 🕐 Daily

Vassos Varoshiotis (££)
This restaurant specialises in fish.
✉ Piale Pashia 7
☎ 2465 5865 🕐 Daily

Protaras

Anemos Beach Restaurant (£)
Good value food served in this taverna in a busy seaside resort .
✉ Fig Tree Bay ☎ 2383 1088
🕐 Daily

Limassol & the South

Avdimou

Melanda Taverna (£)
A good place to have lunch, right by golden sands.
✉ Avdimou Beach ☎ 9942 2233 🕓 Daily

Limassol

Assos Restaurant (££)
A wide range of Cypriot and international dishes.
✉ Amathountos Avenue, Amathus ☎ 2532 1945 🕓 Daily

Blue Island (££)
Excellent *meze*, but good in all respects. Rightly popular with Limassol's well-to-do.
✉ Amathountas Avenue, Amathous ☎ 2532 1466

Floyiera (££)
Good food and occasional live music.
✉ Patron 25, Germasogeia ☎ 2532 5751 🕓 Daily

Glaros Taverna (££)
Taverna in prime setting above the water's edge serving good fish *meze*; cuttlefish in red wine a speciality.
✉ Agiou Antoniou 36 ☎ 2535 7046 🕓 Lunch, dinner. Closed Sat, Sun dinner

Kyani Akti (Blue Coast) (£)
Local fare menu and very good fish.
✉ Georgiou A, Potamos Germasogeia ☎ 2532 2496 🕓 Daily

Lefteris Tavern (£)
Special *meze* and village wine come with Cypriot hospitality in an old style building. Vegetarian dishes can be provided on request if they're not on the menu.
✉ Agios Christinias 4, Germasogeia village ☎ 2532 5211 🕓 Closed Sun

Le Meridien (£££)
Three excellent restaurants serving French and international cuisine.
✉ Old Limassol–Nicosia road ☎ 2563 4000 🕓 Daily

Marios Restaurant No. 2 (££)
Mouthwatering beef and steaks. Additional Italian menu. Very friendly staff.
✉ 8 Stynfalidon, Potamos Germasogeia ☎ 2531 1916 🕓 Daily

Mikri Maria (£)
Unusual and exceedingly small establishment in a backwater, run by two Cypriot women. Vegetarian dishes on request.
✉ 3 Angiras Street ☎ 2535 7679 🕓 Daily

Neon Phaliron (££)
Greek food and a great favourite with the locals for lunch or dinner.
✉ 135 Gladstone Street ☎ 2536 5768 🕓 Closed Wed, Sun evenings

Ladas Old Harbour Fish Restaurant (££)
Big fresh fish cooked on charcoal served in a fine traditional restaurant; very popular with locals. Some fish choices put it into a higher price category.
✉ Old Harbour ☎ 2536 5760 🕓 Daily

Pissouri

Kastro (£)
Good food, friendly service.
✉ Pissouri beach 🕓 Daily

Zygi

Apovathra (££)
Good seafood in a fishing village.
✉ Seafront ☎ 2433 2414 🕓 Daily

Carte Blanche
All attempts will be made to satisfy the faddiest of clients. The menu may include every wonderful item of Greek or Turkish cuisine, but if the customer wants egg and chips or something more obscure, the constituents will be procured, cooked and served with the same flourish as would befit the à la carte menu.

Pafos & the West

Hippo Kebabs
It is thought that when the first settlers came to Cyprus 11,000 years ago they found a ready supply of meat in the form of the pygmy hippopotamus. Although quite agile, it appears that the pig-sized animal was no match for hungry humans, who systematically hunted it to extinction.

Coral Bay
Peyia Tavern (££)
Substantial meals of local dishes.
✉ Main Square, Pegeia
☎ 2662 1077

Pafos
Argo (££)
Delicious moussaka and friendly service.
✉ Pafios Afrodites 21, Kato Pafos ☎ 2623 3327 🕐 Daily

Avgerinos (££)
Individual restaurant with grilled fish dishes.
✉ Minous 4, Kato Pafos ☎ 2693 2990 🕐 Daily

Chez Alex Fish Tavern (££)
Every kind of seafood from red mullet to *kalamari*. Lobster has to be ordered 12 hours in advance.
✉ Constantias 7, Kato Pafos ☎ 2693 4767 🕐 Daily

Devonshire Family Restaurant (£)
A three-course meal complete with a carafe of wine is real value for money. The home-made vegetable soup is delicious.
✉ Diamond Complex, Tafon Ton Vasileon, Kato Pafos ☎ 2694 3197 🕐 Daily

Famagusta Tavern (££)
A variety of traditional dishes including an excellent moussaka. The village wine is surprisingly good.
✉ 1 Kanther Street, Chlorakas ☎ 2627 0948 🕐 Daily

Gorgona Restaurant (££)
Good selection of dishes, prompt service and friendly owner.
✉ Basilica Gardens, Lidas, Kato Pafos ☎ 2693 7181 🕐 Daily

Margarita Inn (££)
For those who appreciate excellent service and quality food.
✉ Margarita Gardens, Kato Pafos ☎ 2694 6927 🕐 Daily

Metaxas (££)
A reputation for succulent steaks.
✉ 8 Amfitrionos, Kato Pafos ☎ 2694 5923 🕐 Daily

Mother's Restaurant (££)
Wide selection of traditional Cypriot dishes and good basic meat meals. Children's menu. The friendly proprietor may well offer sightseeing advice.
✉ Basilica Centre, Apostolou Pavlou Avenue, Kato Pafos ☎ 2693 6474 🕐 Daily

Pandora Gardens Restaurant (££)
Worth visiting for the garlic mushrooms alone.
✉ Byzantium Gardens, Tafon ton Vasileon, Kato Pafos ☎ 2695 0443 🕐 Daily

Ribshack and Indian Restaurant (££)
Generous servings of well prepared international cuisine. Courteous and accomplished owner.
✉ 56 Poseidonos Avenue, Kato Pafos ☎ 2695 4083 🕐 Daily

Polis
Chix Chox (££)
Local and international cuisine, served at relaxed Polis pace.
✉ Plateia Eroon ☎ 2632 2666 🕐 Daily

Ttakas Bay Restaurant (££)
Good location on its private beach and excellent food.
✉ Ttakas Bay on the coast below Neon Chorion village ☎ 2632 1087

Nicosia & the High Troodos

Nicosia

Abu Faysal (££)
Pure Lebanese food enhanced by an attractive garden terrace and mansion-style interior.
✉ **31 Klimentos Street**
☎ **2276 0353** 🕐 **Daily**

Aegeon (£)
Strictly Greek food, tourists welcome but only in ones and twos. Book and record shop attached.
✉ **40 Ektoros Street**
☎ **2243 3297** 🕐 **Dinner only**

Archontikou (££)
Typical local food with outdoor tables.
✉ **Aristokiprou 27, Laiki Geitonia** ☎ **2268 0080**
🕐 **Daily**

Bagatelle (£££)
This is a stylish restaurant for French cuisine at its best, in a nice setting.
✉ **16L Kyriakos Matsis Avenue**
☎ **2231 7870** 🕐 **Mon–Sat**

Corona (££)
This simple restaurant has survived the test of time and continues to serve good traditional food, alfresco in summer.
✉ **Orfeos 15, Agios Dometios**
☎ **2277 4223** 🕐 **Daily**

Erenia (£)
Small establishment with excellent *meze*. Good, firendly atmosphere.
✉ **64a Archiepiskopou Kyprianou Avenue, Strovolos**
☎ **2242 2860** 🕐 **Daily**

Grecos Tavern (£££)
Some unusual dishes and a marvellous vegetarian *meze*.
✉ **3 Menandros Street**
☎ **2267 4566** 🕐 **Mon–Sat, dinner only**

Plaka Taverna (££)
Excellent *meze* in an extremely popular eating establishment. The outside tables in the square are always in demand.
✉ **8 Stylianou Lena Street**
☎ **2235 2898** 🕐 **Daily**

Scorpios (£££)
Excellent French and Cypriot à la carte cuisine with first-class service, a favourite of Nicosians. Cocktail bar upstairs.
✉ **1 Stassinou Street**
☎ **2244 5950** 🕐 **Daily**

Trattoria Romantica (££)
Italian restaurant and steak-house.
✉ **132 Evagoras Pallikaridi**
☎ **2237 6161** 🕐 **Daily**

Kakopetria

Linos Inn/Taverna (£)
A restaurant and inn in a beautifully restored building. Good local food served by friendly staff.
✉ **34 Paleas Kakopetrias Street** ☎ **2292 3161** 🕐 **Daily**

Platres

Kaledonia (££)
Basic but excellent food. *Meze* a speciality.
✉ **Keldonia Building** ☎ **2542 1404** 🕐 **Daily**

Mandra (££)
A village tavern offering the best local dishes, with Greek music and dancing.
✉ **Near centre of Platres**
☎ **2254 2888** 🕐 **Daily**

Psilo Dendro (££)
The grilled trout is good, especially when washed down with a jug of local wine.
✉ **Centre of Platres**
☎ **2542 1350** 🕐 **Daily**

Nineteenth-century Fare
'The principal food of the Cypriotes consists of olives, beans, bread and onions', wrote Sir Samuel Baker in *Cyprus as I Saw It* in 1879. These days a wider range of fare is available, although the olive remains ubiquitous.

The North

Skewer Cuisine
Kebab is a big favourite with the locals. On a summer evening in the suburbs the air is redolent with smouldering charcoal and slowly cooking meat on long skewers. The result is rarely less than delicious for the Cypriots are well practised in this culinary art.

Famagusta (Gazimağusa) Area

Agora (££)
Turkish Cypriot fare; speciality Kup Kebabi cooked in traditional earth ovens.
⊠ **17 Elmas Tabya Sokagi, Famagusta** ☎ **366 5364** 🕐 **Closed Sun**

Akdeniz (£)
Simple local dishes and friendly service.
⊠ **Just north of Salamis Bay Hotel** ☎ **378 8227** 🕐 **Daily**

Cyprus House (££)
Cypriot and international food surrounded by classical relics and objets d'art. There are occassional belly dance performances.
⊠ **Polat Paşa Bulvari, opposite post office** ☎ **366 4845** 🕐 **Lunch and dinner. Closed Sun**

D & B Café Bar (£)
Good snacks in comfortable central location. Movies on Friday evening.
⊠ **Namik Kemal Meydani, opposite Lala Mustafa Paşa Mosque** ☎ **366 6610** 🕐 **Daily from 9AM**

Emir'in Yeri (£)
Turkish Cypriot fare with kebab something of a speciality.
⊠ **Village of Yeniboğaziçi, north of Salamis** ☎ **378 8610** 🕐 **Daily**

Eyva (£)
Good local food with the usual friendly service.
⊠ **Village of Yeniboğaziçi, north of Salamis** ☎ **378 8235** 🕐 **Closed Sun**

Karsel (££)
Traditional fare in pleasant surroundings by the beach.
⊠ **Mağusa Boğazi** ☎ **371 2469** 🕐 **Daily**

Kemal'in Yeri (££)
Fish is the mainstay but the kebab and *meze* are very delicious.
⊠ **Mağusa Boğazi** ☎ **371 2515** 🕐 **Daily**

Kocareis (££)
Beach bar and restaurant, fresh seafood. Next to the Salamis Bay Hotel.
⊠ **Salamis Yolu, Famagusta** ☎ **378 8229** 🕐 **Daily**

Kyrenia (Girne) and Surrounding Area

Açmenya (£)
Simple layout under the stars. Delicious local fare at low cost. Free fruit and coffee.
⊠ **Alsancak village west of Kyrenia on western approach road to Riverside Holiday Village** ☎ **851 8359/821 2736** 🕐 **Daily**

The Address (££)
Full kebab speciality and à la carte restraurant and brasserie. Booking advised.
⊠ **On the seafront on the west side of Karaoglanoglu** ☎ **822 3537** 🕐 **Daily**

Ali Paşa (££)
Overlooking the sea. Friendly reception. Free coffee.
⊠ **Near Lapta** ☎ **821 8942** 🕐 **Daily**

Allahkerim (£)
Good atmosphere, lots of locals and free Turkish coffee.
⊠ **Approx 13km west of Kyrenia to Alsancak** ☎ **821 8957** 🕐 **Daily**

Altinkaya 1 (££)
Renowned for its fish dishes.
⊠ **Towards Lapta, 8km west of Kyrenia** ☎ **821 8341** 🕐 **Daily**

Always Fish Restaurant (££)
Romantic atmosphere at the waterside. The seven-course seafood *meze* is amazing.
✉ Kyrenia Harbour (central) ☎ 852 3893/815 5561 🕓 Daily

The Bamboo (££)
Very good fresh fish and local cuisine.
✉ Alsancak, on the road to Deniz Kizi Hotel ☎ 821 2890 🕓 Dinner. Closed Wed

Baspinar (£)
The view from on high is unrivalled, if you don't get lost en route. Lamb, beef, chicken and fish dishes are on the menu. The speciality on Sunday is young goat stew. Free coffee and brandy.
✉ The heights of Lapta (follow sign posts), west of Kyrenia ☎ 812 8661 🕓 Daily

Birtat (£)
Good local cuisine. Free melon and coffee.
✉ Near Alsancak ☎ 821 1003 🕓 Daily

Canli Balik (££)
Fresh fish and *meze* by the splendid harbour.
✉ Kyrenia Harbour ☎ 815 2182 🕓 Daily 9AM–2PM

Chinese House (££)
As the name suggests, traditional Chinese food.
✉ Kyrenia–Karaoğlanoğlu road ☎ 815 2130 🕓 Dinner daily

Courtyard Inn (££)
Balti/Pakistani alongside European cuisine. Desserts are mouth watering.
✉ Karakum village, about 2km east of Kyrenia ☎ 815 3343/ 815 5566 🕓 Daily

The Crow's Nest (££)
British customers will feel at home with the good pub food and atmosphere in this high mountain village.
✉ Karaman village

☎ 822 2567 🕓 7PM–late. Closed Mon

Erol's (£)
Local kebabs and *meze* cooked on a barbecue.
✉ Ozanköy village ☎ 815 3657 🕓 From 7PM. Closed Sun

The Fireman's Fez (£)
Contemplate the restaurant's name while trying one of the varied traditional courses.
✉ Catalköy ☎ 824 4600 🕓 Daily

Grapevine (££)
International cuisine. Frequented by ex-pats at lunchtimes.
✉ Nicosia Road, Kyrenia ☎ 815 2496 🕓 11AM– midnight. Closed Sun

Happy Garden Restaurant & Bar (£)
No-frills cuisine: speciality firin kebab and slow-cooked meat.
✉ Ozanköy village ☎ 815 3179 🕓 Daily

Harbour Club (£££)
Splendid view over harbour. Two restaurants: upstairs French cuisine and first–class seafood; downstairs typical Turkish dishes.
✉ Kyrenia Harbour (near castle) ☎ 815 2211 🕓 Closed Tue lunch

Hideway Club (££)
Tasty dishes served in a relaxing atmosphere, complete with a pool.
✉ Edremit village, west of Kyrenia, on way to Karaman ☎ 822 2620 🕓 Daily

Jashan (£££)
Indian cuisine and excellent service. Gets busy so booking is advisable.
✉ Edremit village ☎ 822 2514 🕓 Daily from 5PM

Manners Maketh Man
'Do not start to eat before your elders. Always begin your meal by saying grace and eat with your right hand. Do not produce a knife at the table and do not strip a bone clean, do not be too voracious and do not slouch. Do not blow with your mouth over hot food. Eat in a measured manner, for a person should always eat and drink little.' Eleventh-century Turkish etiquette instructions.

Always Room for One More

No Cypriot restaurateur has been known to turn custom away. The place may be packed, but somehow a space will be created, tables and chairs found with the tablecloth going on almost faster than the eye can see.

Kybele (££)
The finest continental and local cuisine.
⊠ Grounds of Bellapais Abbey, Beylerbeyi ☎ 815 7531
⏰ Daily from 11AM

Le Jardin (£££)
Fine cuisine in romantic restaurant with bar.
⊠ Karakum, east of Kyrenia ☎ 854 4398 ⏰ From 7PM. Closed Tue

Laughing Buddha Chinese Restaurant (££)
Authentic Chinese cuisine and a range of specials.
⊠ South of Kyrenia on the Nicosia road ☎ 815 8715
⏰ Lunch and dinner

Lemon Tree (££)
An excellent fish restaurant, also good *meze*.
⊠ Çatalköy Road, 5km east of Kyrenia ☎ 824 4045 ⏰ Daily

Levant Restaurant (££)
Try cold yoghurt soup and tomato sorbet followed by pork with apple and coriander.
⊠ Karaman village
☎ 822 2559 ⏰ Dinner only. Closed Tue

Mardin Fish Restaurant (££)
Good reputation for fish but the shish kebab and *meze* are also worth a try.
⊠ Çatalköy village
☎ 824 4027 ⏰ Daily

Mirabella Restaurant (££)
Good international cuisine.
⊠ 1km outside Kyrenia on the Karakum road ☎ 815 7390
⏰ 7–10.30. Closed Mon

Mountain House Restaurant (££)
Well-prepared international cuisine.

Bellapais Road, Kyrenia
⊠ Bellapais Road, Kyrenia
☎ 815 3881 ⏰ Lunch and dinner. Closed Sat dinner and Sun

Niazi's (££)
Excellent meat dishes; the cooking of kebabs in particular has been turned into an art form.
⊠ West of the harbour, opposite Dome Hotel, Kyrenia ☎ 815 2160 ⏰ Daily

Old Milos (£)
Traditional food in a lovely setting. Not easy to find in the dark, so a daytime reconnoitre advised.
⊠ Alsancak ☎ 821 8939
⏰ Daily

On the Waterfront (£££)
Seaside restaurant with pool and private bay.
⊠ West side of Lapta ☎ 821 8922 ⏰ Lunch and dinner. Closed Thu

Paradise (££)
Specialises in imaginative *meze* and fish and kebab.
⊠ Çatalköy Road, 5km east of Kyrenia ☎ 824 4397 ⏰ Daily

Planters (££)
Splendid colonial house with palm trees. First-class European cuisine. Tea and cakes in afternoon (from 3PM).
⊠ Western end of Karaoğlanoğlu, approx 4.5km west of Kyrenia on main road, inland side ☎ 822 2219/ 853 9499 ⏰ Closed Wed

Rafters (££)
Bistro and pub in what is claimed to be the oldest olive grove in Cyprus. Booking advisable.
⊠ Ozanköy Road, 4km east of Kyrenia ☎ 815 2946 ⏰ 6–1, Sun from 12. Closed Thur

Rose Gardens (££)
Varied food for all tastes.
✉ **Kilicaslan Sokagi, Lapta**
☎ **821 8927** 🕐 **Daily**

Saint Tropez (£££)
Excellent French cuisine in immaculate setting. Booking advised.
✉ **On main road just east of Alsancak** ☎ **821 8324**
🕐 **From 7:30PM. Closed Mon**

Set Fish Restaurant (£)
Excellent seafood of all descriptions at low cost.
✉ **Kyrenia Harbour** ☎ **815 2336** 🕐 **Daily**

Set Ristorante Italiane (££)
Superb courtyard setting with lovely trees. Serves a high quality of food.
✉ **Kyrenia, near mosque on first back street behind harbour**
☎ **815 6008** 🕐 **Closed Mon**

Sevket's (££)
Traditional dishes, fresh fish and vegetarian. Jacuzzi bathing too.
✉ **Lapta, on the main road west of village** ☎ **821 8077**
🕐 **Daily**

Tree of Idleness (££)
Fish and kebab dishes and Turkish Cypriot *meze*.
✉ **Beylerbeyi** ☎ **815 3380**
🕐 **Daily from 11**

Veranda (££)
Seaside restaurant serving local and international cuisine. Booking advised.
✉ **On the eastern side of Karaoğlanoğlu** ☎ **822 2053**
🕐 **From 7PM. Closed Mon**

Yenihan (£)
Very good Turkish fare.
✉ **20 Temmuz Caddesi, Kyrenia** ☎ **815 1276**
🕐 **Daily**

North Nicosia
Moyra (££)
Kebabs, *meze* and steaks in an authentic Cypriot dining room.
✉ **32 Osman Pasa Sokagi, near British High Commission**
☎ **228 6800** 🕐 **11–11**

Pronto Restaurant (£)
Pizzas, steaks and Mexican dishes plus cocktails.
✉ **Mehmet Akif Caddesi, towards the British High Commission, opposite the Government nursery**
☎ **228 6542** 🕐 **Daily**

Saray Hotel (££)
International and Turkish cuisine with an impressive view over the city. Comfortable surrroundings.
✉ **Atatürk Meydani** ☎ **228 3115** 🕐 **Daily**

Güzelyurt (Morfou) Area
Liman Fish and Chips (£)
Uncomplicated menu, but no worse for that and the fish is claimed to be the freshest in Cyprus. Good value for a straightforward meal.
✉ **Gemikonaği near Lefka**
☎ **727 7579** 🕐 **Daily**

Sah's/Güllü (££)
Kebab and excellent *meze*. Live music Wed, Fri, Sat.
✉ **Next to roundabout at entrance to town, approaching from north coast** ☎ **714 3064**
🕐 **Daily, lunch and dinner. Booking advisable Fri, Sat**

Soli Inn (£)
Good stopping place en route to ruins of Soli and Vouni. Varied menu of *meze*, kebabs, *kalamari* and fish.
✉ **West side of Gemikonaği village, west of Güzelyurt**
☎ **727 7575** 🕐 **Daily**

Larnaka & the Southeast

Prices
Prices are per room per night, with breakfast, in high season:

Republic of Cyprus
£   = up to C£40
££ = C£40–C£80
£££ = above C£80

Northern Cyprus
£   = up to TL10,000,000
££ = TL10,000,000– TL20,000,000
£££ = above TL20,000,000

No Room on the Island
In July 1992 Cyprus was said to be full. Leading holiday firms met with the Cyprus tourism authorities to discuss fears that the island would burst at the seams during August. The crisis was brought about by an increase in tourists of 120 per cent.

Agía Napa
Dome Hotel (££)
A large four-star hotel overlooking two long sandy beaches. Lush gardens surround a good-size swimming pool. Food and drink is reasonably priced.
✉ Makronissos ☎ 2372 1006

Grecian Bay Hotel (£££)
Directly overlooking the bay, this top hotel has an unrivalled range of facilities including poolside dining areas and cool mimosa gardens. The hotel also has its own good section of beach.
✉ Agía Napa ☎ 2372 1301

Kermia Beach (£££)
Peaceful self-contained complex of studios and apartments with many facilities. The price is for an apartment for two. Although the buildings are modern, the location is terrific and the atmosphere restful.
✉ 4km east of Agía Napa ☎ 2372 1401

Napa Sol (£)
Modest 35-bedroom hotel. A good-value option for Nissi Beach.
✉ 79 Nissi Avenue ☎ 2372 2044

Nissi Beach Hotel (££)
The first hotel to be built at this little bay, it stands right next to the beach.
✉ Nissi Beach ☎ 2372 1021

Olympic Napa Hotel (£££)
A low-rise building in a quiet location to the west of the resort. The gardens are very pleasant and there is also a children's playground.
✉ Agía Napa ☎ 2372 2500

Larnaka
Faros Village (££)
Bungalow hotel on clifftop near Cape Kition and its light-house.
✉ Perivolia, 14km south of Larnaka ☎ 2442 2111

Flamingo Beach (££)
A modern three-star hotel on the south side of town on the seafront.
✉ Piyale Paşa ☎ 2465 0621

Four Lanterns (Sunotel) (£)
Good town-centre location, on the seafront.
✉ 19 Athinon Avenue ☎ 2465 2011

Lordos Beach Hotel (£££)
Good standard hotel, designed, built and run by the well-known Lordos Group.
✉ Dhekalia Road ☎ 2464 7444

Pavion Hotel (£)
A good choice for the budget traveller, right in the centre of town.
✉ 11 Faneromeni Street, Agios Lazaros Square ☎ 2465 6688

Protaras
Anais Bay Hotel (£)
Small and somewhat intimate, set in gardens close to a beach (normally crowded).
✉ Protaras ☎ 2383 1351

Mimoza Hotel (££)
Relaxed atmosphere and located by a secluded sandy cove. Wide selection of shops, bars and restaurants.
✉ 5km from centre of Protaras ☎ 2383 2797

Pernera Beach Hotel (££)
A medium-size hotel close to a small beach.
✉ Pernera ☎ 2383 1011

Limassol & the South

Rural Hideways

Agro-tourism is the new buzz word for the Cypriot tourist authorities. The plan is to help proprietors renovate traditional houses in the villages to attract a different kind of tourist and spare the remainder of Cyprus the ravages of intensive development.

Limassol
Amathus Beach (£££)
Opulent and well situated, including a Roman tomb in the garden.
 Amathous Avenue
☎ **2532 1152**

Atlantica Bay (££)
Fairly large hotel close to ancient Amathous. Completely refurbished in 1996. A useful feature is the underpass to the beach, cutting out the main road.
✉ **Amathous Avenue**
☎ **2563 4070**

Chez Nous Sunotel (£)
Medium-price and well-run hotel, comfortably smaller than most, with pleasant pool in a leafy garden.
✉ **Potamos Germasogeia**
☎ **2532 3033**

Curium Palace (££)
An older style hotel located in town, and which has maintained high standards over the years. Antique furniture and friendly owner add to the armosphere. The Municipal Gardens with a small zoo are next door.
✉ **2 Byron Street** ☎ **2536 3121**

Four Seasons (£££)
The hotel enjoys a good reputation, the interior design has been considered, and the swimming pool is quite splendid. Thalassotherapy and seaweed treatments are also on offer.
✉ **Old Limassol–Nicosia road, 9km east of town centre**
☎ **2531 0222**

Le Meridien (£££)
Excellent in every respect including splendid indoor and outdoor pools. Sumptuous well-planned rooms and lawns that sweep down to the sea. High quality cuisine is offered in three restaurants with resident band and Cypriot folk evenings.
✉ **Old Limassol–Nicosia road**
☎ **2563 4000**

Miramare Beach Hotel (££)
The hotel was built before the great rush to develop Limassol's eastern coastline. It has become a favourite with British guests over the years. The nightlife of Potamos Germasogeia is close by.
✉ **Potamos Germasogeia**
☎ **2532 1662**

Le Village (£)
Inexpensive and friendly bed and breakfast place.
✉ **242 Leontios A Street**
☎ **2536 8126**

Pissouri
Bunch of Grapes Inn (£)
A restored 100-year-old inn with 11 guest rooms, quite different to the usual modern hotel.
✉ **Pissouri village**
☎ **2522 1275**

Columbia Pissouri Beach (£££)
On its own, right on the fine sandy beach. Impressive Cape Aspro is to the west.
✉ **Pissouri Beach**
☎ **2522 1201**

Accommodation Guide
For the independent traveller the *Cyprus Hotel Guide*, free and published annually by the Tourism Organisation, is invaluable. Every hotel and guest house is listed, giving star rating, number of rooms and price.

Pafos & the West
Nicosia & the High Troodos

Pafos & the West

Agapinor (£)
Excellent small hotel, run by a friendly team.
✉ **26 Nikodemos Mylonas Street, Kato Pafos**
☎ **2693 3927**

Akamas Hotel (£)
Good value small hotel.
✉ **14 Grivas Digenis Street, Polis** ☎ **2693 1521**

Aloe (££)
Medium-size hotel, close to the seafront.
✉ **Poseidon Avenue, Kato Pafos** ☎ **2696 4000**

Annabelle (£££)
Renowned luxury hotel.
✉ **Poseidon Avenue, Kato Pafos** ☎ **2693 8333**

Axiothea (£)
Small hotel between the upper and lower town.
✉ **2 Ivi Maliotis Street, Pafos**
☎ **2693 2866**

Cynthiana Beach (££)
Spectacular location on a rocky shore. Has a small private beach, fairly quiet.
✉ **Kissonerga, 8km north of Pafos** ☎ **2693 3900**

Kings (£)
Small inexpensive hotel near the Tombs of the Kings.
✉ **Tombs of the Kings Road, Kato Pafos** ☎ **2692 33497**

Marion (£)
Long established old style hotel.
✉ **Marion Street, Polis**
☎ **2632 1459**

Paphos Beach (£££)
Enviable beach front location.
✉ **Poseidon Avenue, Kato Pafos** ☎ **2693 3091**

Nicosia & the High Troodos

Averof (£)
A very pleasant hotel, quiet and traditional.
✉ **19 Averof Street, Nicosia**
☎ **2277 3447**

Best Western Classic (££)
Situated just within the walled city, a reasonably convenient location.
✉ **94 Regaena Street**
☎ **2266 4006**

Cleopatra (££)
A popular hotel, centrally located in the new town.
✉ **8 Florina Street**
☎ **2267 1000**

Hilton Hotel (£££)
Nicosia's leading hotel, with a pool and a business centre. The Hilton Hotel was the rendezvous point chosen by the British after the Turkish invasion of 1974, where all British citizens gathered to be taken in convoy to the British Sovereign bases and then out of the country to safety.
✉ **Archbishop Makarios Avenue** ☎ **2237 7777**

Holiday Inn (£££)
Recently refurbished hotel of the international chain.
✉ **70 Regaena Street**
☎ **2266 5131**

Edelweiss (£)
A small pleasant hotel.
✉ **Pano Platres** ☎ **2542 1335**

Makris Sunotel (£)
Nicely situated hotel.
✉ **48 A Mamantos Street, Kakopetria** ☎ **2292 2419**

Troodos Sunotel (££)
High and ideal location for exploring the Troodos.
✉ **Troodos** ☎ **2542 0135**

The North

Famagusta (Gazimağusa) and Surrounding Area

Blue Sea Hotel (£)

Well positioned by the sea for an overnight stay in the Karpasia (► 13). Simple rooms. The owner claims that the fish dinner is 'good fish, big fish, lovely fish. I catch myself', and one can only agree.

✉ **5km southeast of Dipkarpaz village** ☎ **372 2393**

Mimoza Hotel (££)

Located right on the water's edge on a sandy beach, near Salamis.

✉ **Just north of Salamis** ☎ **378 8219**

Salamis Bay Conti Resort Hotel (£££)

Impressive complex of 404 rooms close to the ruins of ancient Salamis. Plenty of facilities on offer.

✉ **11km northeast of Famagusta** ☎ **378 8201**

North Nicosia (Lefkoşa)

Royal (££)

Modern hotel with extensive facilities including a casino, indoor swimming pool, Turkish bath, sauna and massage centre.

✉ **19 Kemal Asik Caddesi** ☎ **228 7621/228 7630**

Saray Hotel (££)

Excellent central location for shopping and sightseeing. High standards make this a popular venue in Turkish Cypriot Nicosia. The balcony of the rooftop restaurant, serving traditional Cypriot and standard European fare, offers terrific views across Nicosia.

✉ **Ataturk Meydani** ☎ **228 3115**

Kyrenia (Girne) and the West

Baspinar (£)

Simple chalets (a total of four) comprising bedroom/living area, kitchenette and bathroom. The complex is adjacent to the Baspinar Restaurant and is over 300m above sea level.

✉ **Lapta, west of Kyrenia** ☎ **821 8661**

British Hotel (£)

Good Kyrenia (Girne) harbour location. There are great views from the restaurant roof terrace.

✉ **Kordonboyu, west end of harbour, Kyrenia (Girne)** ☎ **815 2240**

Dome Hotel (££)

Famous for its colonial past, the longest established hotel in Cyprus occupies a prime position on a rocky outcrop near the harbour. There is a sea water swimming pool, in a natural rocky enclosure to the front of the hotel. The bedrooms are all air-conditioned and there is a casino.

✉ **Kordonboyu Caddesi** ☎ **815 2453**

Dorana Hotel (£)

Situated within easy walking distance of the shopping area and harbour in Kirenia (Girne). Despite the location amid the bustle of the centre, the Dorana is quite peaceful.

✉ **West of the harbour, Kyrenia (Girne)** ☎ **815 3521**

Soli Inn (£)

Seaside hotel near the ruins of Soli, in Güzelyurt Bay.

✉ **Gemikonagi village** ☎ **727 7575**

Picturesque Plumbing

The older Cypriot hotels are known for their erratic plumbing, quite apart from the fact that the drains cannot cope with toilet paper, taps put on the wrong way round, and showers that seem to have been adapted from water cannon are not uncommon.

Souvenir, Handicraft & Leather Shops

Shopping Hours
May–Sept, Mon–Fri 8–1, 4–7, Sat 8–1; Oct–Apr, Mon–Fri 8–1, 2:30–5:30. Shops in tourist areas, north and south, stay open later.

Breaking the Law
All Turkish-made products are banned from the Greek part of Cyprus. Shopkeepers who break the law risk two years in prison or a fine of £1,400. In 1995 Body Shop apologised after Turkish made face flannels were found in one of its shops.

Larnaka and the Southeast
Laïki Geitonia (traditional quarter) is slowly being refurbished in Larnaka at the south end of Zinonos Kiteios Street. 750m to the south on Bozkourt and Ak Deniz streets are a number of pottery shops, including Photos and Fotinis and Stavros. Elenas workshop and Studio ceramics workshop can also be found in this area. Walking about and comparing prices first is a good idea.

The Cyprus Handicraft Service
✉ 6 Kosma Lysioti Street, Larnaka ☎ 2463 0327

Kornos Village
Terracotta pottery is still produced here in the same way as 2,000 years ago.

Liopetri and Xylofagou Villages
Good solidly built baskets are made here.

Melpo Leather and Jewellery
A good selection of both.
✉ 16 Makarios Avenue, Agía Napa ☎ 2372 1226

New Famagusta Leather Shops
Wide range of leather goods for sale.
✉ 2 Makariou, Agía Napa

Photis Tourist Handicraft Centre
A wide range of crafts.
✉ Ileos Pavlou Street, Larnaka

Stavrovouni – Agía Varnava Monastery
A talented monk paints icons to order.

Limassol and the South
A collection of traditional shops by Limassol Castle and others by the old harbour sell pottery and copper goods.

Aspelia Craft
This establishment specialises in high-quality works.
✉ Agora Shopping Centre, junction of Anexartisias and Ágios Andreou streets, Limassol ☎ 2536 4599

Costas Theodorou Ltd
Good quality leather goods at reasonable prices.
✉ 37 Athens Street, Limassol ☎ 2536 3964. Also at 129 Anexartisias Street ☎ 2536 8031

Cyprus Handicraft Centre
Traditional Cypriot handicrafts made in Government-run workshops.
✉ 25 Themidos Street, Limassol ☎ 2530 5118

Lefkara Village (► 49)
A wide range of silverware and lace products can be found on sale in the village. Check that you are being offered the genuine article and not an import.

P and D Mayromatis
Discerning and varied selection of leather goods run by a Cypriot couple who lived for many years in England.
✉ 23 Koumanderis Street, Limassol ☎ 2536 4710

Philips Shoe Factory
Every kind of boot and shoe you can think of, including orthopaedic. Shoes can be specially made to order in two to three days.
✉ Zig Zag Street, Limassol ☎ 2574 8893

Sam's Leatherware
Wide range of goods on sale with leather jackets a speciality.

✉ **1A Anexartisias Street, Limassol** ☎ **2536 2141. Also at 21 Ifigenias Street** ☎ **2574 5156**

Scaraveos Designs
The goods are not exactly arts and crafts but there are some modern and very unusual designs.

✉ **236 Ágios Andreou Street, Limassol** ☎ **2536 0518**

Pafos and the West
Chryssorrogiatissa Monastery
The monks have built up a thriving icon painting business.

Cyprus Handicraft Service
Traditional Cypriot handicrafts made in Government-run workshops.

✉ **64 Apostolou Pavlou Avenue, Pafos** ☎ **2624 0243**

Fyti Village
The villagers produce fine woven cloth, especially embroidered curtains.

Nicosia and the High Troodos
Cyprus Handicraft Centre
The centre was created after the Turkish invasion to provide work for Greek Cypriots displaced from the north. A range of goods are for sale and there is an exhibition of local crafts.

✉ **186 Athalassa Avenue, Nicosia** ☎ **2230 5024**

Another branch of the Cyprus Handicraft Centre is located in Laïki Geitonia, within the walled city.

✉ **Konstantinou Palaiologou Avenue, Nicosia** ☎ **2230 3065**

Foini Village
A reputation for its pottery encourages many to make the long journey to this remote area.

Leventis Museum Gift Shop
Reproductions of historical artefacts, including some attractive jewellery.

✉ **Ippokratous Street (Nicosia walled city)**

Moutoullas
Famed for its bottled drinking water, this mountain village also produces fine wooden basins and copper goods.

Omodos
The tourist trail now takes in Omodos and souvenir shops abound. Examples of traditional embroidery are well worth seeking out.

The North
Ceramic Centre
Largest pottery showroom in the north.

✉ **Ortakoy, 3km northwest of Nicosia** ☎ **223 2302**

Dizayn 74
Pottery made on site while you watch.

✉ **Karaoğlanoğlu Village** ☎ **815 2507**

Estetik
Wide range of leather goods, gifts, decorative household items and a perfumery.

✉ **31–33 Liman Yolu, Gazimagusa** ☎ **366 4064**

Round Tower
Local handicrafts, art and cards.

✉ **Beside the covered market off Kyrenia (Girne) high street** ☎ **815 6377**

Silk Making
Cyprus had, until recently, a great tradition of silk making going back to the Byzantine period. The warm coastal climate and abundance of mulberry trees were ideal for the silkworms and the weaving of silk became a significant cottage industry. Production declined when rural areas turned to the cultivation of lemon groves instead.

Stores, Arcades, Markets & Jewellery Shops

Spectacles Savings
Cypriot opticians have spotted a gap in the spectacle market. They offer special tourist services of a quick turnaround for sight tests and spectacles, all provided at a fraction of the cost at home.

Stores & Arcades

Larnaka and the Southeast
Forum
The store is a relatively modest emporium, perhaps reflecting the lack of competition in Larnaka.
✉ Ileos Pavlou Street, Larnaka
☎ 2465 9200

Woolworth and Super Department Store
A typical department store selling everything from records to jewellery. It also includes a food hall.
✉ General Timagia Avenue
☎ 2463 1111

Limassol and the South
Agora
An impressive modern arcade of 48 shops. Some quality clothes and footwear outlets and a first-rate craft shop.
✉ Junction of Agiou Andreou and Anexartisias streets, Limassol

Marios Shopping Centre
A good range of clothes, shoes, accessories and gifts.
✉ 88 Agiou Andreou Street, Limassol

Marks and Spencer
A visit is guaranteed to make the British visitor feel at home. Useful for forgotten T-shirts.
✉ Makariou III Avenue, Limassol ☎ 2574 8166

Woolworth Olympia
The standard range of department store goods and an in-store food hall and bakery.
✉ 28 Oktovriou Avenue, Limassol ☎ 2559 1133

Woolworth
Not quite the same as in Britain – but not far.
✉ Old Nicosia Road, Limassol (the coast road, 2km east of the zoo and gardens) ☎ 2533 5353

Zako
Famous through Cyprus, this store has not lost the art of selling haberdashery. Browse happily among the buttons.
✉ Koumandaria Street, Limassol ☎ 2536 3644

Pafos and the West
Titania Shopping Arcade
Shopping centres are new to Pafos. This one houses a collection of good shops.
✉ West end of Poseidonos Avenue, Pafos

Woolworth
A very smart store.
✉ West end of Poseidonos Avenue, Pafos ☎ 2694 7122

Nicosia and the High Troodos
Capital Center
This was the first real shopping centre in Cyprus and is still worth a look.
✉ Makarios Avenue, Nicosia, just south of the junction with Evagoras Avenue

City Plaza
The basement is given over to food, then three levels of shops selling clothes, shoes and sportswear.
✉ Makarios Avenue, Nicosia, 60m south of junction with Evagoras Avenue

Marks and Spencer
Modern fashions in this franchise of the British institution.
✉ Makarios Avenue, Nicosia, 40m south of junction with Evagoras Avenue

Woolworth
The store is very popular with the locals and comes complete with self-service restaurant.
✉ **Makarios Avenue, junction with Digeni Akrita** ☎ **2275 8801**

The North
Evkaf Ishani Precinct
✉ **Girne Caddesi**

Galleria Arcade
Two storeys of relatively modern shops.
✉ **Arasta Sokagi**

Markets
Fruit sellers will usually be fairly imprecise about weighing goods, to the customer's advantage. It is common for a few extra plums to be added free of charge.

Larnaka and the Southeast
Municipal Fruit and Vegetable Market
✉ **Ermou Street, Larnaka**

Limassol and the South
Central Market
Fruit and vegetables.
✉ **Saripolou Street, Limassol**

Municipal Market
A wide range of fruit and vegetables.
✉ **Genethliou Mitella Street, Limassol**

Pafos and the West
Municipal Market
Open-air stalls selling fruit and vegetables.
✉ **Pafos lower town, southern end of Fellahoglou Street**

Nicosia and the High Troodos
Municipal Market
✉ **Plateia Dimarchias, Nicosia walled city**

Open Air Market
A splendid place to buy fish, fruit and vegetables, in the shadow of a mosque.
✉ **Constanza Bastion, Konstantious Avenue, Nicosia**

The North
Covered Bazaar
✉ **South side of Selimye Mosque, Nicosia**

Covered Bazaar
✉ **North end of Canbulat Yolu, Famagusta**

Okkes Dayi Market
✉ **Ataturk Caddesi, Kyrenia**

Jewellery Shops

Larnaka and the Southeast
Le Mioneaux
Copies of museum artefacts.
✉ **73 Zinonos Kiteios Street, Larnaka** ☎ **2465 8106**

Santa Maria Jewellery
Gold jewellery on sale and repairs undertaken.
✉ **7 Makariou, Paralimni**
☎ **2382 2284**

Limassol and the South
Bargilis Jewellery
Mainly precious stones.
✉ **72 Athens Street, Limassol**
☎ **2535 4023**

Tonia Jewellery
Gold jewellery a speciality.
✉ **177 Agiou Andreou Street, Limassol** ☎ **2535 5244**

Pafos and the West
Athos Diamond Centre
Hand-made jewellery.
✉ **Poseidonos Avenue, Lighthouse Court 79–80, Pafos**
☎ **2623 4951**

Nicosia and the High Troodos
G Stephanides, Son and Co Ltd
Long-established family business; excellent modern designs.
🌐 **23 Makarios Avenue, Nicosia** ☎ **2275 4419**

Enthusiastic Sales Pitch
Cypriot shopkeepers never admit defeat. If they cannot convince you that the size or colour is just right then your choice will be promised for tomorrow. The promise should not be taken too literally.

Fun Parks &
Go-karting

The Lure of Water
The marinas and waterparks that have sprung up recently in Cyprus almost suggest that previously there was a lack of entertainment for children. Doubtless these expensive ventures will eventually pay off, but the sandy beaches, turquoise seas and swimming pools will always be the better attraction for children. On a cautionary note, as the sun shines fiercely throughout the summer, great care should be taken to avoid a holiday ruined by sunburn.

Larnaka and the Southeast
Agía Napa Luna Parks
There are Luna Parks (fun fairs) with rides and sometimes go-karting in all the major towns. Agía Napa has one adjacent to Waterworld and another about 800m southwest of the monastery.
🖂 **Agía Thekla Road and off Nissi Avenue, Agía Napa** 🕐 **Times vary, but usually daily 9:30–8 (later at weekends)**

Larnaka Luna Parks
There are the usual rides at Larnaka's two Luna parks.
🖂 **Municipal Gardens and on airport road** 🕐 **Times vary, but usually daily 9:30–8 (later at weekends)**

Skycoasters Agía Napa
Amazing death-defying manoeuvres for sober, non-pregnant participants over 1m tall, with no health problems!
🖂 **Adjacent to Luna Park on Nissi Avenue, Agía Napa** 🕐 **Apr–Oct, daily 10–8**

Waterworld Agía Napa
A variety of exciting water chutes, plus log rolling in the activity pool, river trips, spray columns and geysers, and much more. There are also cafés, an ice cream parlour and gift shop, and sculptures in terrific bad taste.
🖂 **5km from Agía Napa along Agía Thekla Road** ☎ **9952 3423/ 9952 3424** 🕐 **Mar–Nov, daily 10–6**

Limassol and the South
Limassol Luna Parks
There are the usual fun-fair rides at Limassol's two Luna parks. The long opening hours are useful for those coming off the beach.
🖂 **Adjacent to the Roussos Beach Hotel and Christaki Kranou Street, Potamos Germasogeia area** 🕐 **Times vary, but usually daily 9:30–8 (later at weekends)**

Nicosia and the High Troodos
Nicosia Luna Park
The usual fun-fair rides, popular for its go-karting facilities. Adults and children can burn off some energy.
🖂 **Vasileos Pavlou Street, Nicosia** 🕐 **Times vary, but usually daily 9:30–8 (later at weekends)**

Tivoli Luna Park
This is a particularly good Luna Park, with a variety of fun-fair rides, adjacent to the International State Fairground. Combine the two venues for an entertaining afternoon away from the beach or as a break from sightseeing.
🖂 **Elia Papakyriakou 10, Engkumi** ☎ **2235 2245/2235 1231/2235 1236** 🕐 **Times vary, but usually daily 9:30–8 (later at weekends)**

Pafos and the West
Pafos Luna Parks
The usual fun-fair rides at the two Luna parks in Pafos.
🖂 **Apostolou Pavlou Avenue and Tourist Office Beach, east of seafront** 🕐 **Times vary, but usually daily 9:30–8 (later at weekends)**

The North
Octopus Aqua Park
Colourful water slides, bouncy castle, pub and restaurant; the only fun park in the north.
🖂 **Catalköy area on the main road, 5km east of Kyrenia** ☎ **0542 8539764** 🕐 **Daily**

Zoos, Rides & Other Activities

Larnaka and the Southeast
Glass-bottomed Boats
See the Mediterranean's aquatic life in its natural habitat and in comfort.
✉ Agía Napa Harbour
☎ 9953 5636 🕓 Summer, daily

Pony Riding
Rides on ponies for children are available in the Troodos Mountains.
✉ Troodos Square 🕓 Most summer days

Limassol and the South
Limassol Reptile House
Native lizards and more exotic creatures, including crocodiles.
✉ Old Harbour, Limassol

Limassol Zoo
Various animals kept in rather cramped conditions. There is also an aviary.
✉ Municipal Gardens, 28 Aktovriou Street, Limassol
☎ 2558 8345 🕓 Daily 9–1, 2:30–6:30

Pafos and the West
Camel Riding
There is occasionally a camel providing rides on the open land at the back of Pafos Harbour.
✉ Behind Pafos Harbour
🕓 Summer, times vary

Glass-bottomed Boats
See the aquatic life of Pafos Harbour.
✉ Pafos Harbour ☎ 9953 5636 🕓 Summer, daily

Kites
The Pafos Municipality organises a kite-flying competition in the Byzantine castle area near the harbour. It takes place in the first or second week in March and is open to all comers. The colourful event is followed by a traditional feast.
✉ Kyriakou Nikolaou Street, Pafos ☎ 2693 2014

Pafos Aquarium
An array of colourful fish from the oceans, seas and rivers of the world. The various fish tanks, one of which contains a pair of small sharks, are built into a series of illuminated caves.
✉ Off Poseidonos Avenue, near Theokepasti Church, Kato Pafos
☎ 2695 3920 🕓 Daily 10–8

Snake George's Reptile Park
Many of Cyprus's reptiles and amphibians belong to threatened species. Snakes in particular, though most are harmless, are often perse-cuted by the islanders. Snake George's Reptile Park aims to give snakes a chance by improving public under-standing and displaying them in their specific natural habitats.
✉ 15km north of Pafos on coastal road to Ágios Georgios, behind BP petrol station
☎ 2693 8160 🕓 Daily 10–sunset

Nicosia and the High Troodos
Ostrich Farm Park
See the fastest two-legged creatures on earth at what claims to be Europe's largest ostrich farm. Visitors can have their photograph taken on an ostrich egg, and there is an exhibition centre, playground and barbecue area.
✉ Ágios Giannis Maloúntas
☎ 2267 4321 (Nicosia office)
🕓 Wed 3–8, Sat, Sun 10–8

Admission Prices
Entry into the Luna parks is free. However, the more innovative and exciting rides/experiences are expensive. Water parks with their impressive features are also expensive. The skycoaster is particularly pricey.

Theatre & Cultural Events

Doubtful Directions
Some of the activities listed on these pages entail trips into the quieter parts of Cyprus. The visitor, if lost or doubtful of the route, should beware of directions given by villagers. They will be anxious to please and in an attempt not to disappoint may assume an unjustifiable knowledge with likely severe inconvenience for the gullible enquirer.

Easter is still the busiest time of year in Cyprus's festival calendar. The pre-Lenten Carnival starts proceedings with 10 days of entertainments and feasting, finishing on Green Monday, an occasion for family picnics in the country. Extravagantly decorated floats parade through Limassol. Green Monday is 50 days before Easter Sunday, and Holy Week begins on Palm Sunday, the Sunday before Easter. Religious icons all over the island are shrouded in black on Maundy Thursday. On Good Friday a solemn mass takes place, followed by a procession in which Christ's image is paraded through the streets. The shrouds are lifted from the icons on Easter Saturday, there are more processions and bonfires and fireworks are lit. Feasting takes place on Easter Sunday.

Larnaka and the Southeast
Agía Napa Festival (September)
In front of the monastery with folk music and dancing.

Larnaka Festival (July)
Dance, theatre and music at the fort and the Municipal Amphitheatre, Artemedos Avenue.
☎ **Further information 2465 7745**

Limassol and the South
Ancient Greek Drama Festival (June–August)
Performances of classical drama are held in the amphitheatre at Kourion and other open-air theatres in the area.

Limassol Festival
Limassol Municipality organises theatre, music and dance events throughout the summer.
☎ **Further information 2536 3103**

Limassol Wine Festival
A very popular event during the first week in September. Music, dance and wine tasting in the Municipal Gardens.

Nicosia and the High Troodos
British Council
Various cultural events in English.
✉ **Museum Street, Nicosia**
☎ **2244 2152**

Goethe Institute
German cultural events.
✉ **21 Markos Drakos Avenue, Nicosia** ☎ **2246 2608**

Municipal Theatre
Regular performances by local and international companies.
✉ **Museum Street, Nicosia**
☎ **2266 9027**

Pafos and the West
Pafos Festival
Pafos Municipality organises theatre, music and dance events throughout the summer at the Odeion Roman theatre and the harbour fort.
☎ **Further information 2692 2804**

The North
A variety of seminars and other cultural events take place throughout the year. Contact the centre in Northern Nicosia for details.
✉ **Attatürk Cultural Centre, northern Nicosia**

Sporting Activities

Angling
Fishing is permitted in 15 dams around the island subject to the purchase of a licence. Licences can be bought from the local Fisheries Department offices. Sea fishing is also possible from all the main coastal resorts.

Specialist angling holidays are also available from the UK. For details contact:
Cyprus Angling Holidays
☎ 01732 450749

Larnarka and the Southeast
Achna Dam
Licences from Larnaka Fisheries Department.
✉ Piale Pashia Avenue
☎ 2463 0294

Limassol and the South
Dipotamos Dam – east of Lefkara
Germasogeia Dam
Kourris Dam
Kalavassos Dam
Lefkara Dam
Licences from Fisheries Department
✉ Limassol Harbour
☎ 2533 0470

Nicosia and the High Troodos
Kafizes Dam
Kalopanagiotis Dam
Lefka Dam
Lympia Dam
Palaichori Dam
Xyliatos Dam

Pafos and the West
Asprokremmos Dam
Mavrokalymbos Dam
Evretou Dam
Licences from Fisheries Department.
✉ Pafos Harbour
☎ 2694 0268

Birdwatching
Cyprus is on the main migration routes for birds coming from Europe to Africa. There are about 98 species resident on the island and 200 more are regular visitors, including 10,000 flamingos who winter on the Salt Lake (► 17). More information is available from:
Cyprus Ornithological Society
✉ 4 Kanaris Street, Nicosia
☎ 2242 0703

Bowling (ten pin)
General information from:
Cyprus Bowling Association
✉ PO Box 5287 ☎ 2435 0085

Limassol and the South
Limassol Bowling
✉ Argyrokastrou Street, Limassol ☎ 2537 0414
🕐 2PM–midnight

Nicosia and the High Troodos
Kykko Bowling
✉ Behind Ledra Hotel, Nicosia
☎ 2235 0085 🕐 1PM–2AM

Cycling
Bikes can be hired in most resorts and the island's terrain is perfect for mountain biking. Sunglasses and hat are advisable in summer.

Cyprus Cycling Federation
✉ PO Box 24572, Nicosia
☎ 2266 3344/2266 3341

Cyprus Mountain Bike Association
For information on mountain biking in the Troodos Mountains, western Cyprus and other rugged areas.
☎ 2235 6174

Shooting
Hunting, mainly the shooting of migratory birds, is a common pursuit in rural areas, much to the despair of environmental groups. Attempts to ban or restrict the annual slaughter have failed to date.

Locals and Swimming
For a long time the local population seemed somewhat baffled by the tourists' passion for the beach. They are coming to terms with the phenomenon, though even now, for most of the year, Cypriots feel that the sea is far too cold to comtemplate swimming.

Cyprus Car Rally
This takes place every year on the last weekend in September and is part of the European Championship. It is one of the toughest courses in the championship with winding dirt tracks and mountain roads.
For information contact:
Cyprus Automobile Association
✉ PO Box 2279, Nicosia
☎ 2231 3233

Diving
There are diving centres and sub-aqua clubs in all the seaside towns and at a number of the larger hotels. Cyprus is surrounded by clear waters, with coral, sponges, sea anemones, shells and colourful fish, giving great views to divers.

Football
There is a local league with 90 teams in four divisions and there are football pitches in all the main towns. There are also four teams that compete on an international basis.
KOP (Cyprus Football Federation)
☎ 2235 2341

Limassol and the South
Tsirio Stadium Limassol
International matches

Golf
This is a relatively new sport to Cyprus but there are now three golf courses on the island.

Pafos and the West
Tsada
18-hole course, set in the grounds of a 12th-century monastery, in a valley. Facilities include a restaurant, tennis and outdoor pool.
✉ North of Pafos ☎ 2664 2774

Secret Valley
18-hole course, set in a scenic valley surrounded by rock formations.
✉ East of Pafos, near Petra tou Romiou ☎ 2696 83900

Pareklissa
9-hole course.
✉ Elias Beach Hotel, east of Limassol ☎ 2532 5000

Hang-gliding
This takes place in the Kyrenian Hills and is promoted by the North Cyprus Turkish Aviation Association, based at Nicosia Airport.

Horse Racing

Nicosia and the High Troodos
Meetings are held at weekends throughout the year; on Sunday afternoon from January to mid-May and September to December, and on Saturday afternoon from mid-May to the end of July.

Nicosia Racecourse
✉ St Paul's Street, west of the city centre ☎ 2237 9566

Horse Riding

Limassol and the South
Elias Beach Horse Riding Centre.
Lessons are available, with headgear provided. Trekking can be enjoyed in nearby countryside.
✉ 8km east of Limassol
☎ 2532 5000 ext 317

Nicosia and the High Troodos
Lapatsa Sports Centre
Headgear and footwear sold at the centre's shop. A selection of horses and ponies. Tuition in dressage and cross-country.
✉ Near Pano Deftera
☎ 2262 1201

Pafos and the West
Pafos Riding Centre
✉ Near Tombs of The Kings.

George's Range
✉ Coral Bay–Ágios George road, near Pegeia ☎ 2662 1790

Sailing

Larnaka and the Southeast
Larnaka Nautical Club
☎ 2462 3399

Larnaka Marina
Facilities for visiting yachts.
☎ 2465 3110

Limassol and the South
Limassol Nautical club
☎ 2532 4282

St Raphael Harbour
✉ Limassol ☎ 2532 1100

Pafos and the West
Pafos Nautical Club
☎ 2694 3700

The North
Kyrenia (Girne) Harbour
A shelter for yachts touring the southern Mediterranean.
✉ Kyrenia Harbour

Dolphin Sailing
Dinghies, parasailing, speed-boat and aqua-rocket trips.
✉ Denis Kizi beach, near Kyrenia ⏱ May–Oct

Shooting
General information on all the clubs is available from:
Cyprus Shooting Association
✉ PO Box 12681, Nicosia
☎ 2248 6673

Larnaka and the Southeast
Famagusta District Shooting Club
Larnaka Shooting Club
✉ 4km northwest of the city centre at Kamares
☎ 2453 0309 ⏱ Wed,, Sat

Limassol and the South
Limassol Shooting Club
✉ Near Polimidia, 8km northwest of city centre on the Troodos road ☎ 2565757
⏱ Tue–Sun

Nicosia and the High Troodos
Nicosia Shooting Club
✉ 8km southeast of the city centre ☎ 2248 2660
⏱ Tue–Sun

Pafos and the West
Pafos Shooting Club
✉ 12km east of Pafos on Old Limassol Road ☎ 2626 2109
⏱ Wed, Sat

Skiing

Nicosia and the High Troodos
Mount Olympus
The season is January until March. Four runs of about 200m in Sun Valley. Five longer, more demanding runs on the north face. Two tracks for cross-country skiers. Equipment can be hired in Sun Valley. Mount Olympus is 3km from the Troodos hill resort and an hour drive from Limassol and Nicosia.

Skiiers Dilemma
Skiing enthusiasts have a dilemma. At weekends they need to get to the ski shop early before the best gear is given out, but if there has been overnight snow they will be lucky to get their cars up the last section of Mount Olympus if they beat the snow plough. Another reason for getting on the slopes early is that the snow soon turns to mush in the mid-morning heat. Powder snow is a rarity.

Sporting Activities & Walking

Water-skiing
Discounts can be negotiated for the promise to turn up every day. However, almost certainly the boat will be broken down, or elsewhere when it is wanted. In addition an eye should be kept on the time allocation, for mysterious laws of relativity tend to make the driver's watch run faster than the skiers.

Swimming
The extensive coastline offers excellent opportunities for swimmers. Red buoys indicate swimming areas. Most beaches offer safe bathing, but some beaches in the Pafos area can be dangerous in rough weather and warning notices must be heeded. Part of the beach at Kourion, clearly marked, is also unsafe for bathing.

Larnaka and the Southeast
Larnaka public beach
There are changing facilities and a café on site. Free entry.
✉ **10km east of Larnaka**
☎ **2464 4511**

Limassol and the South
Dhassoudi public beach
There are changing facilities and a café on site. Free entry.
✉ **5km east of Limassol**
☎ **2532 2811**

Pafos and the West
Geroskipou
Changing facilities and café on site. Free entry.
✉ **3km east of Pafos**
☎ **2623 4525**

Swimming Pools

Nicosia and the High Troodos
Nicosia Olympic Pool
On the west side of the town, near the General Hospital.
✉ **Loukis Akritas Avenue**
☎ **2277 4472** 🕐 **May–Oct**

Limassol and the South
Limassol Pool
Next to Dhassoudi beach.

Larnaka and the Southeast
Larnaka Pool
Municipal sports centre in the middle of the town.

Pafos and the West
Pafos Pool
Northeast of the old town.
☎ **Agiou Dionysiou Street**

Water Sports
Swimming, diving, sailing, windsurfing and water-skiing are possible at all the resorts, south and north.

Tennis
There are tennis courts in most of the larger hotels and municipal courts in the main towns.

Walking
Midsummer is much too hot for this pastime – even the mountain temperatures prove too high for most people. As a result, many visitors to Cyprus are enthusiastically turning to walking in the cooler months. Cypriots, however, remain to be converted: the idea that anyone would wish to travel more than a short distance on foot for pleasure is incompre-hensible to many.

Consequently, until recently at least, there were no ramblers' paths or trails. Any routes discovered had a strictly utilitarian purpose related to farming or hunting and rarely went where the rambler wished to go.

There are numerous oppor-tunities for walking in the mountains. The best large-scale maps are the British Ministry of Defence series. Try the Department of Lands and Survey in Nicosia for copies (☎ 2280 5504).

In the north walkers will have problems with access as many of the mountain areas are closed off due to the presence of the military.

All walkers should remember that even at high altitude the weather can be very hot and that anyone undertaking a strenuous walk or climb should take water with them.

Conversely, those walking in winter should realise that many of the mountains are very high and that bad weather is common and they should dress accordingly.

Nicosia and the High Troodos

There are four walking trails in the Troodos region. These have been designed by the Cyprus Tourism Organisation (CTO), which provides helpful leaflets listing all the flora, geology and other natural items of interest.

The trails themselves are not always that well marked on the ground, and the tourist office leaflet is not as detailed as it could be. Walkers therefore need to keep their wits about them and rely on their initiative at times.

Forest roads abound. They are gouged out of the hillside regularly by the Forestry Department and are every-where in the Troodos Mountains.

For most walkers they are really something of a last resort as they generally follow every twist and turn of the contour line they happen to be on, resulting in about two kilometres travelled for every genuine kilometre gained.

Artemis Trail

The trail is named after Artemis (Diana), the ancient goddess of forests.

A high-level circuit of 6.5km around Mount Olympus starts a short distance up the main road to the summit.

Atalante Trail

The trail is named after the mythological forest nymph. Starts from Troodos Post Office and is 9km long.

After about 3km from the start point the trail reaches a spring of clean drinking water. There are wooden benches at various points along the way.

Kaledonia Trail

This is also known as 'the trail of nightingales' due to its warbling birds. The start is reached by turning off the Platres road heading down to the summer presidential residence.

The trail runs along the banks of the river to the falls and is 3km long. In summer this cool ravine is refreshing, and thick shade is provided by trees.

Persephone Trail

This trail is named after the goddess of spring. It offers beautiful scenery. It starts just south of Troodos Square and is about 6.5km there and back.

Pafos and the West
Akamas Trails

In the Akamas there are two trails. Both start from the Baths of Aphrodite and both are about 7.5km long, initially heading west of the Baths before going their separate ways (► 16).

Countryside Care

You are kindly requested not to litter the countryside, cut flowers or plants, or damage structures. Such actions contravene the Forest Law and offenders face prosecution.

What's On When

Traditional Festivals

The Greek Cypriots have a wealth of traditional festivals and fairs. Many derive from the Greek Orthodox Church, others have distant pagan origins. Despite this rich heritage the number of events grow. There are now beauty contests, Olympic Day 10km runs, beer festivals, dog shows and annual exhibitions of coinage.

January

New Year's Day (1 Jan)
Epiphany (6 Jan): one of the most important Greek Orthodox religious celebrations of the year

March

Greek National Day (25 Mar): parades and celebrations

April

National Day (1 Apr): anniversary of the EOKA uprising
Turkish Children's Festival (23 Apr)

May

Labour Day (1 May)
May Fair in Pafos (1 May): 10 days of cultural events and exhibitions of Cypriot flora, basketwork and embroidery
Anthestiria Flower Festivals (early May): the festivals' origins go back to celebrations honouring the god Dionysos in ancient Greece
Turkish Youth Festival (19 May)
Cyprus International Fair (late May): the largest trade fair in Cyprus, held in Nicosia and lasting 10 days

July

Larnaka Festival (throughout Jul): performances of dance and theatre in the fort and the Pattichon amphitheatre

August/September

Turkish Communal Resistance Day (1 Aug)
Turkish Victory Day (30 Aug)
Limassol Wine Festival (late Aug–first week in Sep): a 12-day festival, with music and dance some evenings

October

Independence Day (1 Oct)
Greek National Day (28 Oct): also known as Ochi Day.

Student parades all over southern Cyprus
Turkish National Day (29 Oct)

November

Proclamation of Turkish Republic of North Cyprus (15 Nov)

December

Christmas Day (25 Dec)

Moveable Feasts

Apokreo Festivities (50 days before Orthodox Easter): two weeks of fun in most towns. Limassol has fancy dress balls and children's parades.
Green Monday (50 days before Orthodox Easter): a day of laughter, funny disguises and vegetarian picnics in the country.
Procession of Ágios Lazaros Icon, Larnaka (eight days before Orthodox Easter Sun): a special mass service in memory of Ágios Lazaros followed by an impressive procession carrying his icon through the town
Easter: the biggest Greek Orthodox religious feast – on the Sunday, celebrations last all day
Kataklysmos, Festival of the Flood (50 days after Easter, coinciding with Pentecost): celebrations take place in all the seaside towns and include dancing, folk singing, swimming competitions and boat races
Agia Napa Festival (late Sep): a weekend of folk music, dance and theatre, combined with agricultural exhibitions
Seker or Ramazan Bayram: a three-day feast at the end of the Ramadan fast
Kurban Bayram: four days during which lambs are traditionally sacrificed and shared with the needy

Practical Matters

Above: *Limassol beach*
Right: *bust of Athenian Kimon at Larnaka*

117

TIME DIFFERENCES

GMT
12 noon

Cyprus
2PM

Germany
1PM

USA (NY)
7AM

Netherlands
1PM

Spain
1PM

BEFORE YOU GO

WHAT YOU NEED

	UK	Germany	USA	Netherlands	Spain
● Required / ○ Suggested / ▲ Not required — Some countries require a passport to remain valid for a minimum period (usually at least six months) beyond the date of entry – contact their consulate or embassy or your travel agent for details.					
Passport/National Identity Card	●	●	●	●	●
Visa (► 119, Arriving. Check regulations before your visit to Cyprus.)	▲	▲	▲	▲	▲
Onward or Return Ticket, Republic of Cyprus	●	●	●	●	●
Onward or Return Ticket, North Cyprus	▲	▲	▲	▲	▲
Health Inoculations	▲	▲	▲	▲	▲
Travel and Health Insurance (► 123, Health)	○	○	○	○	○
Driving Licence (national with English translation or International)	●	●	●	●	●
Car Insurance Certificate (if own car)	●	●	●	●	●
Car Registration Document (if own car)	●	●	●	●	●

WHEN TO GO

Coastal Cyprus

High season

Low season

JAN	FEB	MAR	APR	MAY	JUN	JUL	AUG	SEP	OCT	NOV	DEC
17°C	17°C	19°C	23°C	26°C	30°C	32°C	33°C	31°C	27°C	22°C	19°C

Very wet · Wet · Cloud · Sun

TOURIST OFFICES

In the UK
Cyprus Tourist Office
17 Hanover Street
London W1R 0AA
☎ 020 7569 8800
Fax: 020 7499 4935

Northern Region of
Cyprus Tourist
Information Office
29 Bedford Square
London WC1B 3EG
☎ 020 7631 1920
Fax: 020 7631 1948

In the USA
Cyprus Tourism
Organisation
13 East 40th Street
New York
NY 10016
☎ 212/683 5280
Fax: 212/683 5282

Northern Region of
Cyprus Tourist
Information Office
1667 K Street, Suite
690, Washington
DC 20006
☎ 202/887 6198
Fax: 202/467 0685

POLICE 112 (Republic)	155 (North)
FIRE 112 (Republic)	199 (North)
AMBULANCE 112 (Republic)	112 (North)
FOREST FIRES 1407 (Republic)	

WHEN YOU ARE THERE

ARRIVING

The national airline, Cyprus Airways (☎ 2266 3054) operates scheduled flights from Britain and mainland Europe to Larnaka and Pafos. There are no direct flights to North Cyprus: you fly via Turkey, for which you need a visa if you intend visiting.

Larnaka Airport
Kilometres to city centre

5 kilometres

Journey times	
🚆	N/A
🚌	30 minutes
🚗	20 minutes

Ercan Airport
Kilometres to Nicosia

23 kilometres

Journey times	
🚆	N/A
🚌	35 minutes
🚗	15 minutes

MONEY

The currency of the Republic of Cyprus is the Cyprus pound (C£), divided into 100 cents. Coins are in denominations of 1, 2, 5, 10, 20 and 50 cents; notes C£1, 5, 10 and 20.

The currency of North Cyprus is the Turkish lira (TL). Coins are TL100, 500, 1,000, 2,500, 5,000, 10,000, 25,000 and 50,000; notes TL10,000, 20,000, 50,000, 100,000, 250,000, 500,000, 1,000,000 and 5,000,000.

TIME

 Cyprus is two hours ahead of Greenwich Mean Time (GMT+2), but from late March, when clocks are put forward one hour, to late October, summer time (GMT+3) operates.

CUSTOMS

 YES

Goods Obtained Duty Free taken into Republic of Cyprus (Limits):
Alcohol (over 22% vol): 1l
Wine: 0.75l
Cigarettes: 200 or
Cigarillos: 100 or
Cigars: 50 or
Tobacco: 250g
Perfume and Toilet Water: 300ml (not more than 150ml of perfume)

Goods Obtained Duty Free taken into North Cyprus (Limits):
Alcohol (over 22% vol): 1.5l and Wine 1.5l
Cigarettes: 400 or
Cigarillos: 200 or
Cigars: 100 or
Tobacco: 500g
Perfume: 100ml
Toilet Water: 100ml

You must be 18 and over to benefit from the alcohol and tobacco allowances.

 NO
Drugs, firearms, ammunition, offensive weapons, obscene material, unlicensed animals, fruit, nuts, vegetables, cut flowers, bulbs and seeds.

HIGH COMMISSION/EMBASSIES/CONSULATES

UK	**Germany**	**USA**	**Netherlands**	**Spain**
2247 3131/7 (RoC)	2244 4362/3 (RoC)	2247 6100 (RoC)	2536 6230 (RoC)	2243 3151 (RoC)
227 4938 (NC)	227 5161 (NC)	225 2440 (NC)		

WHEN YOU ARE THERE

TOURIST OFFICES

Republic of Cyprus

● Cyprus Tourism
  Organisation
  Leoforos Lemesou 19
  PO Box 24535
  CY 1390 Nicosia
  ☎ 2233 7715
  Fax: 2233 1644

● Aristokyprou 11
  Laïki Geitonia
  CY 1011 Nicosia
  ☎ 2267 4264

● Spyrou Araouzou 115A
  CY 3036 Limassol
  ☎ 2536 2756

● Georgiou A' 22
  CY 4040 Germasogeia
  ☎ 2532 3211

● Plateia Vasileos Pavlou
  CY 6023 Larnaca
  ☎ 2465 4322

● Gladstonos 3
  CY 8046 Pafos
  ☎ 2693 2841

● Léoforos Kryou Nerou 12
  CY 5330 Agía Napa
  ☎ 2372 1796

● CY 4820 Platres
  ☎ 2342 1316

● Agiou Nicolaou 2
  CY 8820 Polis
  ☎ 2632 2468

North Cyprus

● Nicosia
  ☎ 227 9112 or 228 9629

● Kyrenia
  ☎ 815 2145/815 2227

● Famagusta
  ☎ 366 2864

OPENING HOURS REPUBLIC

○ Shops   ● Archeological Sites
● Offices   ○ Museums
● Banks   ○ Pharmacies

| 9AM | 10AM | 11AM | 12PM | 2PM | 3PM | 4PM | 5PM | 6PM |

☐ Day   ☐ Midday
☐ Evening

In addition to the times above, offices, shops and pharmacies close Wednesday and Saturday PM. Afternoon hours are 2:30 to 5:30 (offices 3 to 6) October to April. Banks open 8:15 July, August, Monday 3:15 to 4:45 all year. Banks in main tourist areas open afternoons. Most museums close for lunch and also one day a week.

OPENING HOURS NORTH

○ Shops   ● Archeological Sites
● Offices   ○ Museums
● Banks   ○ Pharmacies

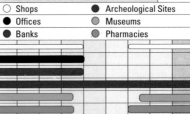

| 9AM | 10AM | 11AM | 12PM | 2PM | 3PM | 4PM | 5PM | 6PM |

☐ Day   ☐ Midday
☐ Evening

In addition to the times above, shops and pharmacies open 8 to 1 and 2 to 6 in winter and shut Saturday PM in summer. In winter offices open 8 to 1 and 2 to 5; banks open 8 to 1 and 2 to 5; museums open 8 to 1 and 2:30 to 5.

DRIVE ON THE
LEFT

TOILETS
CHARGE

★ ★
★ ★

PUBLIC TRANSPORT

 Regional Buses Republic of Cyprus: Intercity and village buses operate frequently between towns and various holiday resorts with many trips per day. Almost all villages are connected by local buses to nearest towns but services operate only on weekdays once a day leaving early in the morning, returning to the villages in the afternoon.

North Cyprus: Except for the main routes such as Nicosia to Kyrenia, buses are infrequent and do not run to a timetable and your fellow passengers are more likely to be soldiers than tourists.

 Boat Trips Republic of Cyprus: One-day boat excursions (including lunch) operate from May to October. Popular trips include: Limassol harbour to Lady's Mile Beach; Pafos Harbour to Coral Bay and Pegeia; Agía Napa to Paralimni and Protaras coast; Larnaka Marina along Larnaka, Agía Napa and Protaras coast; and Latsi along the Akamas coast.

North Cyprus: From May to October there are boat trips (including lunch) from Kyrenia Harbour to the beaches at Acapulco or Mare Monte (☎ 815 3708).

 Urban Transport Republic of Cyprus: Urban and suburban buses operate frequently only during the day (starting very early in the morning) between 5:30AM and 7PM. During summer, in certain tourist areas, buses may operate until midnight. It is a good idea to check routes with your hotel.

North Cyprus: There is a good bus service within the main towns, with buses running approximately every half hour. Check with your hotel for more detailed information.

CAR RENTAL

 Many firms, including the internationally known, though mainly local ones in the north. Cars are expensive in the Republic, cheap in the north. Drivers must usually be between 25 and 75 and have had a license for over a year.

TAXIS

 In the Republic service taxis, shared with other people (4 to 7 seats) operate between main towns every half hour. There are also rural taxis that operate in hill resorts and urban taxis in towns. In the north taxis can only be found at taxi stands.

DRIVING

 Speed limits on motorways and dual carriageways: **100kph; min 65kph (North Cyprus: 60mph)**

 Speed limits on country roads: 80kph **(North Cyprus: 40mph)**

 Speed limits on urban roads: 50kph, **or as signposted (North Cyprus: 30mph)**

Must be worn in front seats at all times and in rear seats where fitted.

 Random breath-testing. Limit: 39 micrograms of alcohol (59 north) in 100ml of breath.

Petrol in the Republic of Cyprus costs as much as any in Europe. In the north it is cheaper. Grades sold in the south are super, regular, unleaded and diesel. In the north unleaded petrol is not sold. Petrol stations in the south are open 6AM–6PM, closing 4PM Saturdays, many on Sundays. In the north they may open until 9 or 10PM.

 If you break down in the Republic of Cyprus 24-hour towing facilities are provided by the Cyprus Automobile Association in Nicosia (☎ 2231 3131), which is affiliated to the Alliance International de Tourisme (AIT).
If the car is hired follow the instructions given in the documentation.

PERSONAL SAFETY

The police are relaxed and helpful and English is widely spoken. In tourist areas in the south Cyprus Tourism Organisation representatives can provide a degree of assistance. However, crime in Cyprus is at a reassuringly low level. Any problem is more likely to come from visitors. Take the usual precautions with regard to handbags and valuables left in cars. Any thefts or offences should be reported to the police, if only for insurance purposes.

- Do not cross the Green Line (the dividing line between the two parts) except on a day trip from Nicosia south to the north.

- Keep away from military zones (north or south).

- Do not use roads marked as blocked-off on a map (they may encroach on military zones).

Police assistance:
☎ **112 (Republic)**
☎ **155 (North)**
from any call box

TELEPHONES

In the Republic public telephones are found in town centres. They take 2, 5, 10 and 20-cent coins or *telecards* (C£3, C£5, C£10, from banks, post offices, tourist offices or kiosks). In the north public phones are scarce. They take tokens (*jetons*) or *telekarts*, sold at Telekomünikasyon offices.

International Dialling Codes

From Cyprus to:

UK:	00 44	**Germany:**	00 49
USA:	00 1		
Netherlands:	00 31		
Spain:	00 34		

POST

Post Offices
There are main post offices in main towns and sub-post offices in the suburbs.
Republic: open Mon–Fri 7:30–1:30 (Thu also 3–6).
☎ 2230 3219
North: open Mon–Fri 8–1, 2–5, Sat 8:30–12:30.
☎ 228 5982

ELECTRICITY

The power supply is: 240 volts

Type of socket: Square, taking three-square-pin plugs (as UK). In older buildings, round two-pin sockets taking two-round-pin (continental-style) plugs.

TIPS/GRATUITIES

Yes ✓ No ✗		
Restaurants (if service not included)	✓	10%
Cafés (if service not included)	✓	10%
Hotels (if service not included)	✓	10%
Hairdressers	✓	50p/£1
Taxis	✓	10%
Tour guides	✓	50p/£1
Cinema usherettes	✗	
Porters	✓	50p/bag
Cloakroom attendants	✓	50p
Toilets	✗	

PHOTOGRAPHY

What to photograph: landscapes, picturesque villages, bustling towns, flowers and wildlife.

Where it is forbidden to photograph: in both north and south near military camps or other military installations, in museums, and in churches with mural paintings and icons where flashlight is required.

Where to buy film: the most popular brands and types of film can be obtained from shops and photo laboratories. Film should not be bought from kiosks as it may well have been 'roasted'.

HEALTH

Insurance
Tourists get free emergency medical treatment; other services are paid for. For UK nationals benefits are available in the Republic by arrangement with the Department of Health before departure. Medical insurance is advised for all.

Dental Services
Dental treatment must be paid for by all visitors. Hotels can generally give recommendations for local dentists. Private medical insurance is strongly advised to all tourists to cover costs of dental treatment in Cyprus.

Sun Advice
Cyprus enjoys almost constant sunshine throughout the year. Wear a hat and drink plenty of fluids during the hot months (particularly July and August) to avoid the risk of sunstroke. A high-protection sunscreen is also recommended.

Drugs
Minor ailments can be dealt with at pharmacies (*farmakio* in the south, *eczane* in the north). Pharmacies sell all branded medicines. Some drugs available only on prescription in other countries are available over the counter in Cyprus.

Safe Water
Tap water in hotels, restaurants and public places is generally safe to drink though not very palatable in the north, particularly around Famagusta where the sea has invaded boreholes. Bottled water is cheap and widely available.

CONCESSIONS

Students Cyprus is not really on the backpacker route, but there are youth hostels in Nicosia, Larnaka, Pafos, Agía Napa and in the Troodos Mountains. For details contact: The Cyprus Youth Hostel Association, PO Box 21328, CY 1506 Nicosia (☎ 2267 0027). There is a Youth Card available that offers a range of discounts. Contact the Cyprus Youth Board, Lefkosia, Themistokli Dervi 41, Hawaii Tower ☎ 2230 4160/5, fax 2245 5135.

Senior Citizens Few concessions are made to elderly visitors. Most hotels offer discounts during the low tourist season, but you do not have to be a senior citizen to take advantage.

Cyprus/Europe	UK	USA	Rest of Europe	
46	36	36	46	
48	38	38	48	
50	40	40	50	
52	42	42	52	
54	44	44	54	
56	46	46	56	Suits
41	7	8	41	
42	7.5	8.5	42	
43	8.5	9.5	43	
44	9.5	10.5	44	
45	10.5	11.5	45	
46	11	12	46	Shoes
36	14	14	36	
37	14.5	14.5	37	
38	15	15	38	
39/40	15.5	15.5	39/40	
41	16	16	41	
42	16.5	16.5	42	
43	17	17	43	Shirts
34	8	6	36	
36	10	8	38	
38	12	10	40	
40	14	12	42	
42	16	14	44	
44	18	16	46	Dresses
38	4.5	6	38	
38	5	6.5	38	
39	5.5	7	39	
39	6	7.5	39	
40	6.5	8	40	Shoes

WHEN DEPARTING

- Remember to contact the airport or airline 72 hours prior to leaving to ensure flight details are unchanged.
- Departure tax is included in the cost of an airline or ferry ticket in the Republic but in the north a tax of 1,000,000 Turkish lira is payable upon departure.
- Items of antiquity may not be taken out of Cyprus.

LANGUAGE

Cyprus has two official languages, Greek and Turkish. Greek is spoken in the Republic of Cyprus and Turkish in the north. Most Greek Cypriots speak good English but an attempt at the language is useful, for example in a village coffee shop and similar places where locals may not know English. In the north things are different – not as much English is spoken. Waiters and others have only a limited fluency and some knowledge of Turkish is a definite advantage. Below is a list of some words that you may come across.

English	Greek	Turkish
hotel	*xenodhohío*	*otel*
room	*dhomátyo*	*oda*
... single/double	*monó/dhipló*	*tek/iki kishilik*
breakfast	*proinó*	*kahvalti*
toilet	*twaléta*	*tuvalet*
bath	*bányo*	*banyo*
shower	*doos*	*dus*
balcony	*balkóni*	*balkon*
bank	*trápeza*	*banka*
exchange office	*ghrafío sinalághmatos*	*kambiyo bürosu*
post office	*tahidhromío*	*postane*
money	*leftá*	*para*
cash desk	*tamío*	*kasa*
credit card	*pistotikí kárta*	*kredi karti*
traveller's cheque	*taxidhyotikí epitayí*	*seyahat çeki*
exchange rate	*isotimía*	*döviz kuru*
restaurant	*estiatório*	*restoran*
café	*kafenío*	*bar*
menu	*menóo*	*menü*
lunch	*yévma*	*ögle yemegi*
dinner	*dhípno*	*aksam yemegi*
dessert	*epidhórpyo*	*tatli*
waiter	*garsóni*	*garson*
the bill	*loghariazmós*	*hesap*
aeroplane	*aeropláno*	*uçak*
airport	*aerodhrómio*	*havaalani*
bus	*leoforío*	*octobüs*
... station	*stathmós*	*otogar*
boat	*karávi*	*gemi, vapur*
... port	*limáni*	*porto sarabi*
ticket	*isitírio*	*bilet*
... single/return	*apló metepistrofís*	*tek gidis/gidis dönüs*
yes	*ne*	*evet*
no	*óhi*	*hayir*
please	*parakaló*	*lütfen*
thank you	*efcharistó*	*tesekkür ederim*
hello	*yásas, yásoo*	*merhaba*
goodbye	*yásas, yásoo*	*hosça kal*
sorry	*signómi*	*özür dilerim*
how much?	*póso?*	*ne kadar?*
I (don't) understand	*(dhen) katalavéno*	*sizi anliyorum*

INDEX

Acknowledgements
The Automobile Association wishes to thank the following photographers, libraries and associations for their assistance in the preparation of this book:
HULTON GETTY 14; MARY EVANS PICTURE LIBRARY 10, 76b; MRI BANKERS' GUIDE TO FOREIGN CURRENCY 119; PA NEWS 11; SPECTRUM COLOUR LIBRARY 57, 86.
The remaining photographs are held in the Automobile Association's own picture library (AA PHOTO LIBRARY), with contributions from:
MALC BIRKITT 5b, 7, 9b, 13, 19, 23, 26, 27a, 33, 34, 43, 45, 49b, 50, 54, 59, 60, 61, 68, 73, 76a, 78, 117a, 117b; ROBERT BULMER 24, 25, 75, 80, 83; ALEX KOUPRIANOFF 1, 2, 5a, 9a, 9c, 12, 15a, 15b, 16, 17, 18/19, 20, 21, 22, 28/9, 31, 35, 37, 38a, 38b, 39a, 48, 52, 56, 62, 64a, 65a, 67, 70, 72, 77, 79, 81, 87, 88, 90, 91a, 91b; ROY RAINFORD 6, 8b, 27b, 41, 44, 47, 49a, 58, 64b, 66; H ULCAN 85.

Author's Acknowledgements
Robert Bulmer acknowledges the invaluable contribution of his daughter, Fiona Bulmer, in the preparation of this book. Thanks also to John Wood, General Manager of Le Meridien Hotel, Limassol for his generous assistance and to Holiday Autos International Ltd of Frimley, Surrey for arranging jeep hire.

Contributors
Updater (2002): George McDonald Page Layout: Design 23 Indexer: Marie Lorimer
Revision Management: Outcrop Publishing Services Limited, Cumbria

Dear Essential Traveller

Your comments, opinions and recommendations are very important to us. So please help us to improve our travel guides by taking a few minutes to complete this simple questionnaire.

You do not need a stamp (unless posted outside the UK). If you do not want to cut this page from your guide, then photocopy it or write your answers on a plain sheet of paper.

Send to: **The Editor, AA World Travel Guides, FREEPOST SCE 4598, Basingstoke RG21 4GY.**

Your recommendations…

We always encourage readers' recommendations for restaurants, nightlife or shopping – if your recommendation is used in the next edition of the guide, we will send you a *FREE* AA *Essential* **Guide** of your choice. Please state below the establishment name, location and your reasons for recommending it.

_____

_____

_____

_____

Please send me **AA *Essential*** _____

(*see list of titles inside the front cover*)

About this guide…

Which title did you buy?

AA *Essential* _____

Where did you buy it? _____

When? m m / y y

Why did you choose an AA *Essential* Guide? _____

_____

_____

_____

_____

Did this guide meet your expectations?

Exceeded ☐   Met all ☐   Met most ☐   Fell below ☐

Please give your reasons _____

_____

_____

_____

continued on next page…

Were there any aspects of this guide that you particularly liked? _____

_____

_____

_____

Is there anything we could have done better? _____

_____

_____

_____

_____

About you...

Name (*Mr/Mrs/Ms*) _____

    Address _____

_____

_____ Postcode _____

    Daytime tel nos _____

Which age group are you in?

    Under 25 ☐ 25–34 ☐ 35–44 ☐ 45–54 ☐ 55–64 ☐ 65+ ☐

How many trips do you make a year?

    Less than one ☐ One ☐ Two ☐ Three or more ☐

Are you an AA member? Yes ☐ No ☐

About your trip...

When did you book? m m / y y   When did you travel? m m / y y

How long did you stay? _____

Was it for business or leisure? _____

Did you buy any other travel guides for your trip?

    If yes, which ones? _____

_____

Thank you for taking the time to complete this questionnaire. Please send
it to us as soon as possible, and remember, you do not need a stamp
(*unless posted outside the UK*).

Happy Holidays!